Sunset Travel Guide to
NORTHERN CALIFORNIA

By the Editors of Sunset Books and Sunset Magazine

Lane Books · Menlo Park, California

PHOTOGRAPHERS

Edited by Elizabeth Hogan

Third Printing August 1971

CONTENTS

SPECIAL FEATURES

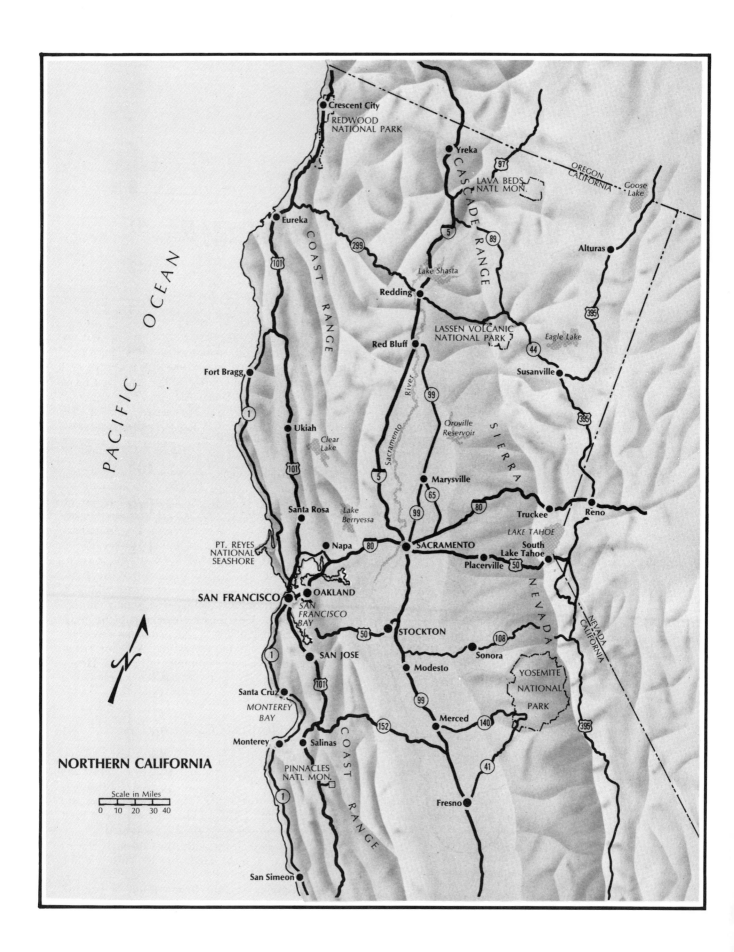

NORTHERN CALIFORNIA

Scale in Miles
0 10 20 30 40

EXPLORING NORTHERN CALIFORNIA

Northern California, with its varied climate and terrain, offers vacationers a wide range of activities. You can fish, hike, and camp in the mountains or relive the past at a ghost town in the Sierra foothills. You can beachcomb along the coast or stroll through stately redwood groves. San Francisco provides big-city activities.

This *Travel Guide to Northern California* contains information on exploring both the well-established and well-known attractions and lesser known but equally appealing spots.

San Francisco, famous for its bay, bridges, hills, views, waterfront, and fine food, is Northern California's most populated city and biggest tourist attraction. Along with the surrounding Bay Area, this is also Northern California's largest cultural, business, and industrial center.

The state capital, Sacramento, is the main city in the agriculturally important Central Valley. Sacramento is currently undergoing a rigorous redevelopment program, scheduled for completion by the end of the 1970's, creating cultural and trade centers and recreating an Old Sacramento. To the east of the Valley lie the Sierra foothills and remnants of the days when gold ruled the lives of Californians.

Other popular destinations in Northern California are Sonoma with its Spanish landmarks, the Napa Valley with its vineyards and wineries, Monterey with its historical buildings and waterfront, Carmel with its quaint shops, and Mendocino with its arts and crafts atmosphere and dramatic coast. Those who prefer the less visited areas head for the Northern Mountains, above Redding, where lonesome roads lead to small villages. The most visited spots for outdoor recreation are Lake Tahoe, Yosemite National Park, Lake Shasta, and the coast redwood parks.

The area covered in this book differs from the southern part of the state in climate, history, topography, and temperament; for that reason separate books are devoted to exploring Northern California and Southern California. The boundary line that we have used to divide the state begins at the ocean near San Simeon, continues across the Coast Range and the southern tip of the Central Valley, and then turns northward across the Sierra Nevada range south of Yosemite National Park. The area south of this dividing line is described in the Sunset book, *Travel Guide to Southern California*.

Climate and terrain

Northern California has three distinct climate zones. Coastal temperatures are mild the year around; rarely will there be extremes in temperature. Fog frequently blankets the coast during the summer, especially in the morning and evening, and in the winter it rains.

As you move inland, the seasons become more pronounced. Summers become hotter (with relatively little humidity), winters colder (with only an occasional snow). The Sierra Nevada has the most dramatic seasonal changes—the summer days are warm, ideal for outdoor recreation. Autumn brings a crispness to the air and dramatic fall colors. Heavy snowfalls during the winter make the mountains a mecca for skiers.

Driving in Northern California

Most major highways carry a heavy flow of traffic, especially near a major city and especially during the morning and evening commute hours. California's roads are well maintained; most thoroughfares are divided four-lane highways. The highway speed limit is a maximum 65 miles per hour or as posted.

The most scenic north-south route through Northern California is State Highway 1. This winding coastal route overlooks the ocean most of the way. Drive it leisurely; take the inland routes if you are in a hurry. U.S. Highway 101, State Highway 99,

TALL, SLIM CONIFERS grow among the jagged mountain peaks of the Sierra Nevada. Here you can find solitude in the wilderness.

COIT TOWER stands atop San Francisco's Telegraph Hill.

and Interstate 5 are the faster north-south routes. The most heavily traveled east-west routes are U.S. Highway 50 and Interstate 80, which connect the San Francisco Bay Area and Lake Tahoe.

When driving in the mountains during the winter, carry tire chains.

Accommodations

Major cities and resort areas usually have plenty of hotel and motel space. However, if you want to stay at a particular place, or if you are traveling during the summer or on a weekend, it is best to make advance reservations.

If you are uncertain of places to stay, write to local chambers of commerce. They usually have listings of accommodations available.

Camping

If you plan to camp in a state park, there is a 7 to 15 day camping limit during the heavy-use period (usually June 1 to the end of September). During the

rest of the year, the limit is 30 days. Camping fees are based on the type of campsite: $1 to $2 for unimproved; $3 for improved (restrooms, hot and cold running water, laundry room, showers), and $3.50 with trailer hookups. For a pamphlet listing California's state parks, write to the Department of Parks and Recreation, P.O. Box 2390, Sacramento 95811.

Though reservations are not required to camp at a state park, some of the state parks do accept them. It is best to have a reservation if you plan to camp at a state park near a metropolitan area during the summer or on weekends. For a reservation form, write to the San Francisco Maritime State Historical Monument, 2905 Hyde Street, San Francisco 94109. Send the completed form to the Department of Parks and Recreation in Sacramento. Reservations must be received at least two weeks in advance.

To camp in a national park or forest, there is a charge of $1 per day. Campsites are available on a first come, first served basis. For a listing of national forest campgrounds, write to the U.S. Forest Service, 630 Sansome Street, San Francisco 94111. For information on national park campgrounds, write the

ANCIENT REDWOODS (Sequoia sempervirens), *found along northern coast, are preserved in numerous parks.*

ROCKY HEADLANDS are typical of northern coast. Ocean here is good for fishing, dangerous for swimming.

National Park Service, P.O. Box 36063, San Francisco 94102.

Northern California also has numerous county and private campgrounds. For a listing of private as well as public campgrounds, see the Sunset book, *Western Campsite Directory*.

The length of the camping season depends upon the location of the campsite. At some places you can camp the year around; however, campgrounds generally are open from June through Labor Day.

Hunting and fishing

Rules governing the hunting season and the animals you may hunt change from year to year. The Department of Fish and Game, 1416 9th Street, Sacramento 95814, publishes a pamphlet every May which lists the current hunting regulations.

The Department of Fish and Game also publishes a pamphlet every May regarding both fresh-water and salt-water fishing regulations.

Both of these booklets, as well as hunting and fishing licenses, can be obtained at sporting goods stores.

Boating

Boating on Northern California's waters is under the jurisdiction of the Department of Harbors and Watercraft in Sacramento. The main boating areas are Lake Tahoe, Lake Shasta, Clear Lake, Lake Berryessa, and the Delta. The best map of public and private boating areas and facilities available is published by the Automobile Club of Southern California. Members of the American Automobile Association can obtain this map—*Boating Recreation in California*—at any AAA office in California.

Winter sports

The Sierra Nevada is the main winter sports area in Northern California. There are several major ski resorts around Lake Tahoe. Other skiing centers are in the Donner Summit area, along U.S. Highway 50 and Interstate 80, and at Yosemite National Park.

Mt. Shasta, north of Redding, offers a long skiing season; and there is also skiing at Lassen Volcanic National Park.

SAN FRANCISCO

Chinatown • Golden Gate Park • North Beach
Fisherman's Wharf • Ghirardelli Square

Powell and Geary streets

San Francisco is unique—it is a big city without being big. Its total area geographically is only 47½ square miles, its population less than 800,000; however, it has the diversity of activities, the hustle-and-bustle, the rich historical background, and the elusive thing known as *atmosphere* that are found in all of the world's great cities.

San Francisco has a look of its own. It is a city noted for its many and various-sized hills and spectacular sweeping views. The skyline reveals new skyscrapers dwarfing once-tall buildings, while a closer look shows crowded row houses and apartments marching endlessly up and down the hills.

San Francisco is one of the world's most visited cities. Whether the visit is your first or fifth, you will enjoy seeing the old establishments as well as browsing around the new.

The climate

The water which surrounds San Francisco on three sides keeps it air-conditioned the year around. The average high is 70° and the low 50°. Fog is frequent in early morning and evening, especially during the summer months. Usually the rains begin in November and last into April. September is usually San Francisco's warmest month.

San Francisco's continual mild temperatures call for light-weight wools at any time of the year. Usually a coat is needed in the evening. Natives tend to shy away from casual clothes and dress conservatively, especially downtown.

Driving in the city

San Francisco's steep hills are part of the city's charm, but they are frequently somewhat disconcerting to the out-of-town visitor. If you are a stranger to steep hills, or if you just don't like city driving, you will probably enjoy your sightseeing more if you do not drive. The downtown area is best explored on foot, and you can use public transportation to get to other points of interest.

If you do drive the hills, have confidence in your car and take it slowly downhill. Remember to shift into low *before* you start up or down a hill.

San Francisco law requires you to curb your front wheels every time you park on a hill. Failure to do so

Hyde Street

Row Houses on Mason Street

will result in a ticket and a fine. The city also has a strict "tow-away" law. Signs in certain areas tell you very clearly that if you park between certain hours (usually 7 to 9 A.M.; 4 to 6 P.M.) Monday through Friday your car will be towed away.

Many of San Francisco's streets are one way, and they don't always fit into a predictable sequence. Watch carefully for the one-way signs.

The cable cars

Riding a cable car is a must for every visitor. It is an excellent means of transportation in the most heavily congested part of the city, and the ride will provide thrills and good views.

There are three cable car lines—two that run on Powell Street and one on California Street. Cars from the lines on Powell Street leave from the turntable at Powell and Market and are spectacular hill climbers. They take you steeply up Powell, then down and around several sharp turns to arrive in 15 or 20 minutes at their respective turntables at the north waterfront. Cars marked Powell and Market/ Bay and Taylor clang through a section of North Beach and the edge of Chinatown and come to the end of their line at Bay and Taylor at Fisherman's Wharf. The cars marked Powell and Market/Hyde and Beach bypass most of Chinatown and North Beach. But they take you down Hyde for a magnificent view of the bay and a hang-on-tight ride to the turntable below Hyde and Beach at Aquatic Park.

The red-painted cars of the California Street line leave from California and Market and take you through the financial district and Chinatown, up steep Nob Hill, and finally down a more gentle grade to the end of the line at Van Ness Avenue.

A cable car ride is 25 cents, and a bus or street car transfer is given upon request. On Sundays and certain holidays you can purchase a 50-cent all-day excursion ticket and ride wherever you please on any municipal bus, street car, or cable car.

There is no easy way to board a cable car. Usually more people are waiting to ride than there is room for. When the car stops, step right up to find a place to ride. If you are on the outside, hang on and be careful.

For a close look at how a cable car works, visit the Cable Car Barn at Mason and Washington (you pass it on the Bay/Taylor cable car line) which houses the power system. Built around 1878, the barn was recently restored and refurbished to include a gallery and museum.

The barn is open daily from 8 A.M. to midnight. The first cable car is on display as are some historic photographs of San Francisco. You can also watch giant 14-foot wheels wind the cable which provides power for the system.

Buses and street cars

San Francisco's buses and street cars run frequently and on an efficient schedule from morning through early evening. You will find a route map and a description of the routes at the front of the yellow section of the San Francisco phone directory.

The city's municipal railway system (buses, cable cars, street cars) operates an information service. If you call 558-4111, the information center will tell you which line to take to reach your destination.

Local buses and street cars are 20 cents a ride. Drivers do not carry change, so have the exact fare ready.

On weekdays from 10 A.M. to 3 P.M. "shoppers' shuttle buses" run at 5-minute intervals through the downtown shopping district. These buses fly yellow flags and charge only 10 cents a ride.

STEP RIGHT UP when cable car stops, usually in intersection. You can ride inside or out.

There also are express buses. They make limited stops and may take you right by your destination. Fare is 25 cents.

Taxicabs

Taxicabs are more numerous than in most other Western cities, and as distances between San Francisco's main points of interest are frequently short, taxis are popular.

Sightseeing tours

If you prefer to take a guided tour of San Francisco, Gray Line offers several different ones. You can make arrangements to be picked up at your hotel, or you can board a shuttle bus at Union Square, opposite the St. Francis Hotel, which will take you to the depot. Buses leave from First and Mission streets at the East Bay Bus Terminal.

There are a number of sightseeing companies that offer limousine tours for small groups. Make arrangements through your hotel or check the classified section of the telephone directory.

FORTY-NINE MILE DRIVE

This scenic drive is a good way to grasp the city as a whole, and then you can return to explore on foot the places which interest you the most. The drive is well marked by blue, white, and orange seagull signs and is easy to follow, although it does take you through the most congested streets of the downtown area. You should allow about half a day to fully enjoy the sights along this route.

You can begin anywhere, but Civic Center at Van Ness Avenue and McAllister Street is a good starting place. The public buildings are clustered around spacious Civic Center Plaza, beneath which are an underground exhibit hall (Brooks Hall) and a three-story garage (entrance on McAllister). Dominating the group is the City Hall, a splendid edifice of granite surmounted by a lofty dome rising 300 feet above the ground. Other buildings include the State Building, Public Library, Federal Office Building, Civic Auditorium, Veterans' Memorial Building (the San Francisco Museum of Art is on the top floor), and the Opera House. On Golden Gate Avenue is the 21-story Federal Courthouse and Office Building which occupies an entire block and towers over the lower buildings of Civic Center.

The signs of the Drive lead you along Van Ness Avenue to the city's automobile row, and then right on Geary Street to the downtown area. You pass Union Square, heart of the shopping district, and then follow narrow auto, truck, and pedestrian-choked Grant Avenue north through Chinatown.

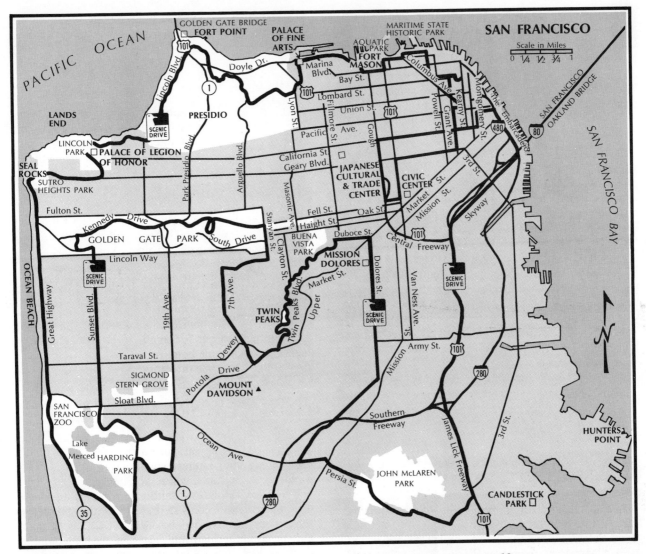

Heavy line designates scenic 49-Mile Drive. For detailed map of downtown area, see page 18.

Where Columbus Avenue crosses Grant on the diagonal, you come to new territory. To the west is the North Beach area—San Francisco's Italian community, its Bohemia, a region of numerous good restaurants, and a lively center of night life.

You continue on Grant to Lombard, where you climb to the top of Telegraph Hill for spectacular views of the city and the Golden Gate and Bay bridges. From here, the seagull route takes you down to the north waterfront area. In a mile or so, you come to the residential district called the Marina, with a bay view out to the Yacht Harbor across the invitingly open stretch of Marina Green—a favorite place for San Franciscans to fly kites, walk their dogs, sun bathe, or just watch the activity on the bay.

Depending on the day, you will have a splendid view of the orange-red Golden Gate Bridge stretching itself in the sun, or just a glimpse of the bridge towers through the fog.

Just to the south down Baker Street, you will see the graceful dome of the Palace of Fine Arts, now the Palace of Arts and Science. The Palace, in its lovely setting on a quiet lagoon, was designed as a "temporary" structure for the 1915 Panama Pacific International Exposition—but San Franciscans could never bring themselves to tear it down. In 1967 the Palace was completely restored and now houses an Exploratorium, a museum of science and technology.

Next you will enter the gates of the venerable Presidio, an active military post since 1776. Inside, you drive past the approach to the Golden Gate Bridge, through stands of eucalyptus, cypress, and pine, and around the northwestern cliffs and beaches. You pass through Lincoln Park (where the California Palace of the Legion of Honor, one of the city's three art museums, is located), swing around to Geary Boulevard, and on to Point Lobos Avenue where the successor to the original Cliff House stands. Behind

CLIFF HOUSE, at northern end of Great Highway, is perched on rocky point battered by ocean waves.

MISSION DOLORES, where city began, maintains humble appearance next to neighboring church.

this restaurant are Seal Rocks. From August to May you can see and hear the sea lions who inhabit the craggy rocks about 400 feet off shore.

Just up the hill in charming little Sutro Heights Park, a few crumbling statues still stand in the once grand estate of Adolph Sutro, whose money came from silver in the Comstock Lode. Here is the best view of Ocean Beach.

The Drive follows the Great Highway for three miles along Ocean Beach to the San Francisco Zoo. It then swings inland around Lake Merced, passes San Francisco State College, and heads north to wind through Golden Gate Park.

Your next major stop is at Twin Peaks, for the most encompassing view of the city. Then the Drive dips down to Mission Dolores. Established in 1776, the Mission was the sixth in the California chain. Its ceilings are decorated with Indian art, and the original bell and altar from Mexico still remain. Be sure to walk through the garden cemetery, where you'll see the final resting places of many San Francisco pioneers and some early Mexican and Irish settlers. An impressive statue of Father Junipero Serra stands in the courtyard.

From here the Drive takes you south around John McLaren Park, then follows the James Lick Freeway back toward the downtown area. It leaves the freeway at Bryant Street and takes you through an industrial area, along the Embarcadero, and past the Ferry Building at the foot of Market Street.

The Ferry Building stands as a reminder of the days when traffic across the bay was entirely by ferry. Even after the bay was bridged, thousands of commuters continued to pour through the old building until the last of the Southern Pacific ferries made its final trip in 1958. Now the building is partially obscured by the double-decked Embarcadero Freeway that skirts this section of San Francisco's waterfront. In the north wing of the Ferry Building, the World Trade Center displays the goods of over a hundred importers and exporters.

Tapes for tours

Tape-recorded commentaries are now available if you want some guidance while sightseeing in the city. You take the portable tape player in your car, or carry it over your shoulder if you are walking.

Auto-Tape Tour at 325 Mason Street follows the 49-mile sightseeing route and provides a map, driving instructions, and general information. Info-Tape offers a narrative for walking as well as driving. The walking trip covers Nob Hill, Chinatown, the financial district, and North Beach, while the driving tour goes along part of the 49-Mile Drive. The office is at 225 Powell Street. Auto Adventures Tape Tour, c/o Nob

DOME of San Francisco's city hall dominates Civic Center complex.

PALACE OF FINE ARTS, on Baker Street, stands majestically behind quiet lagoon. It is sole survivor of 1915 Pan Pacific Exposition.

Hill Travel Lobby, of the Fairmont Hotel, covers sections of the 49-Mile Drive, suggests three side trips, and provides a guidebook and map.

The tour offices are open from 9 A.M. to 6 P.M. daily. For weekend rentals it is advisable to call ahead to reserve a tape. Rental fees range from $2.85 to $4.85 per day.

DOWNTOWN

Downtown San Francisco, unlike the "downtowns" of so many cities, is concentrated within a fairly small area, making it relatively easy to explore on foot. Contained in this section of the city are shops and department stores, theaters, restaurants, the principal business district, and a number of San Francisco's leading hotels.

Leave your car in a downtown garage and use public transportation to reach areas not within walking distance.

Union Square

For browsing and shopping in the downtown area, Union Square makes an ideal starting point. You can park your car in the vast garage beneath the square—it goes down four floors and provides places for over a thousand cars.

Stop first at the square itself. On a nice day, its benches will be lined with people relaxing in the sun or feeding the hundreds of pigeons that swirl about and congregate around the feet of anyone who offers a handout.

Union Square is a center of activity, hosting fashion shows, rallies, and concerts. In spring, Rhododendron Days are celebrated, and huge tubs of the colorful plants are placed throughout the square. A summer activity is the Cable Car Bell Ringing Contest.

In the center of the square stands a 97-foot granite monument commemorating Admiral Dewey's victory at Manila Bay during the Spanish-American War.

The fashionable St. Francis Hotel is on the west side of the square, across Powell Street. Many visiting dignitaries stop here—if you see a foreign flag displayed above the entrance, it is honoring a special guest from that particular country.

Post, Stockton, and Geary streets also border the square. Here, and spreading south toward Market and east toward Kearny are some of San Francisco's smartest shops.

You can't miss the colorful sidewalk flower stands. They are a kind of street-side almanac: sprigs of daphne in spring, tiny Pinocchio roses in summer, chrysanthemums in fall, and holly in winter.

On the east side of the square across Stockton is Maiden Lane, a two block tree-lined alley of interest-

DAFFODIL FESTIVAL signals arrival of spring. Annual event is held in two-block-long Maiden Lane.

ing shops. Of particular interest is a building designed by Frank Lloyd Wright, with an unusual yellow brick front and an interior circular ramp. It houses a gallery.

In early April, Maiden Lane ushers in spring with the annual Daffodil Festival. The lane is then closed to traffic, and local dignitaries, bands, troubadours, and lots of blossoms are on hand.

More smart shops and large department stores are located along Grant Avenue and Kearny. Of special interest is the floral shop of Podesta Baldocchi. The floral decorations in its windows and inside the shop are indeed remarkable; visitors are welcome.

Also a major attraction in the Union Square area is Gump's on Post near Stockton. It is noted especially for its Jade Room which contains an amazing jade collection of all known shades. Other rooms contain rare imports and unusual locally made items.

Market Street

The streets of the Union Square area all lead to Market Street, the wide, busy thoroughfare that runs diagonally across the city from Twin Peaks to the Ferry Building. The strip of Market just south of Union Square is a continuation of the downtown shopping area.

At Powell and Market is the turntable for the Powell Street cable cars. The route ends here, and the cars are spun around to head again for the north waterfront.

Several long blocks west of this intersection is the Fox Plaza, a 29-story building which combines apartments with businesses. Here is the office of the San Francisco Visitors and Convention Bureau which provides tourist information upon request. Just to the north is the Civic Center complex.

Where Geary, Kearny, and Market streets converge you will see Lotta's Fountain, a reminder of Lotta Crabtree who charmed San Franciscans during the Gold Rush days.

At Market and New Montgomery stands a San Francisco landmark, the Sheraton-Palace Hotel. It is a magnificent eight-story structure with a reputation for grandeur which began with its opening in 1875. The original building, built by silver king William Ralston, was severely damaged in the 1906 earthquake-fire. In 1909 reconstruction was completed, and the hotel reopened for business. The glass-roofed Garden Court dining room is a fine example of the elegance of old San Francisco.

Market Street is achieving a new look through the addition of high-rise buildings and beautifully landscaped plazas. The Crocker Building, at Post, Montgomery, and Market, towers 38 stories above a landscaped square. At 555 Market you can stroll through the colorful gardens at the Standard Oil Company Plaza. On the ground floor of this 43-story building visitors can view an exhibit on the history of petroleum.

The impressive 20-story, green glass monolith of the Crown-Zellerbach building rises above a pleasantly landscaped park at the corner of Market and Bush. At noon this plaza is a favorite gathering place of downtown office workers. Just north of the eastern end of Market is the Golden Gateway, a recent redevelopment project. High-rise apartment buildings, townhouses, shopping areas, and parks comprise about 3 square blocks. Of particular interest is the Alcoa Building with its patterned facade of exposed diagonal bracings.

Market Street is undergoing an additional beautification program in conjunction with the advent of Bay Area Rapid Transit. The BART trains will run underneath Market, and a minimum of traffic will flow on the street itself. The sidewalks will be widened, and rows of trees will line the street. Old-fashioned street lamps will continue to light the street after dark. This beautification program is a long range project, but should be completed in the early 1970's.

The financial district

North of Market Street, impressive office buildings shade the narrow slot formed by Montgomery Street, heart of San Francisco's business and financial district. Here, and spreading into the nearby streets, are the banking, brokerage, and insurance firms that are a part of the Wall Street of the West. Here also are the general offices of many of the West's largest business organizations.

The heart of the financial district is the Pacific Coast Stock Exchange (Pine and Sansome) where business begins early in the morning so as to coincide with the hours of the New York Exchange. From the visitors' gallery you can see the trading floor—in the center is a telegraph operator's booth, and a machine spews out a continuing serpentine of ticker tape. If you turn on one of the listening boxes in the gallery, you will hear a brief explanation of how business is transacted and coordinated between two floors (San Francisco and Los Angeles) 400 miles apart. You can visit the Exchange from 9 A.M. to 1:30 P.M. Monday through Friday. Guided tours are given to groups of visitors.

One block west of the Stock Exchange is the headquarters for the world's largest bank, Bank of America. Now the tallest building in San Francisco at 52 stories and 770 feet, the bank, with its bronze-tinted bay-windowed facade, covers most of the California, Pine, Kearny, and Montgomery block. A magnificent view can be had from the public restaurant on the 52nd floor.

The city's second tallest skyscraper, the Wells Fargo Building at 44 Montgomery, rises 43 stories and 561 feet. On the 16th floor of this unusual glass and steel structure is Montgomery Lane where a variety of shops open onto a mall-like area with benches, canopies, and a brick walkway. Just below the main lobby level is a restaurant that displays early California artifacts from the Wells Fargo History Room. The History Room is located at 420 Montgomery. Here you will see a varied collection of objects important in the history of the West, including a stagecoach dating back to around 1860 which ran south of San Francisco over the Santa Cruz Mountains. Visitors are welcome Monday through Friday from 10 A.M. to 3 P.M.

Chinatown

The largest Oriental community outside the Orient, San Francisco's Chinatown covers about 24 blocks and is roughly bordered by Kearny, Mason, and Bush

BANK OF AMERICA *building towers above other downtown skyscrapers.*

ROAST DUCK, a Chinese delicacy, hangs in window of Chinatown market.

ROLL OF DRUMS on Grant Avenue signals Chinese New Year Parade. Annual event, held in January or February, draws tremendous crowds.

streets, and Pacific Avenue. The best way to arrive in Chinatown is on foot or by public transportation, as the area is heavily congested with traffic. You can walk to Grant Avenue, the main street, from either the financial district, Union Square, or Nob Hill. Remember that if you are atop a hill, your walk will be down several steep blocks. The California Street Cable Car will put you in the heart of Chinatown.

One of the most colorful approaches to Chinatown is a walk down Sacramento to Grant. You will see peaked rooftops and bright-colored balconies in the foreground, and the bay and bridge beyond. If you walk along Grant Avenue, you will see the tourists' Chinatown—curio shops, import stores, restaurants.

To get the non-tourist glimpse, prowl up and down some of the cross streets and side alleys that parallel Grant. Scattered among gift shops and restaurants are stores and markets with exotic smells and sounds.

Between California and Pine is St. Mary's Square, a quiet little park with Beniamino Bufano's striking marble and stainless steel statue of China's one-time President Sun Yat-sen. Dr. Sun stands with a block-long row of poplars at his back. Beneath the park is an underground garage; entrances are on Kearny, Pine, and California.

Old St. Mary's Church, a San Francisco landmark since 1854, stands at Grant and California. The Gothic structure was built of brick brought around Cape Horn from New England and granite from China.

Just east of Grant Avenue, at Kearny and Clay, is where San Francisco began. Here Captain John B. Montgomery raised the American flag in 1846 proclaiming the Mexican village to be a possession of the United States. Portsmouth Plaza (named for Montgomery's ship the *USS Portsmouth*) today is a landscaped park atop a parking garage. Among the pines is the first memorial to American author Robert Louis Stevenson, who during his visits to San Francisco spent considerable time at the Plaza.

From Portsmouth Plaza you can cross a walking bridge east over Kearny Street to the dramatic A-frame Chinese Cultural and Trade Center. This 27-story structure includes an exhibition hall for Chinese art, an auditorium, a Chinese library, meeting halls, and a hotel.

The Chinese Telephone Exchange at 743 Washington, now the Bank of Canton, is a Chinatown landmark. The building once held the main switchboard for the "China" exchange, when Chinese operators memorized as many as 2400 names and numbers of

Chinatown subscribers. You can see photographs of the ladies at the Chinese Historical Museum on Adler Place, an alley one half block south of Broadway off Grant Avenue. On display are memorabilia covering a century of Chinese life in America. The museum is open Tuesday through Sunday from 1 to 5 P.M. Admission is free.

THE CITY'S HILLS

San Francisco is famous for its many hills and the views which each affords. Some hills are more accessible than others (only a footpath reaches the summit of Mount Davidson), some are more interesting physically, and some provide exceptional views. Nob, Telegraph, and Russian hills, and Twin Peaks are probably San Francisco's most popular.

Nob Hill

To reach the top of this hill take the California or Powell Street cable car. Or if you prefer to drive, there are several parking garages on California Street, close to Mason.

The very top of the hill covers about three square blocks. Before the earthquake and fire of 1906, this small hilltop was the site of the city's grandest mansions. Only one still survives: the imposing brownstone built by James C. Flood. Now the Pacific Union Club, it faces California, just west of Mason.

Two of San Francisco's most famous hotels, the Fairmont and the Mark Hopkins, stand atop Nob Hill at California and Mason. The luxurious Fairmont, the tallest building on the hill, has several restaurants, a spacious lobby, and a cocktail lounge at the top. You can reach the Crown Room in an outside glass-walled elevator, or if you prefer in an inside elevator.

Across California Street is the Mark Hopkins Hotel, long known for the elegant Top of the Mark cocktail lounge. Panoramic views can be had from both the Crown Room and the Top of the Mark.

Two blocks west, at California and Jones, is the very Gothic Grace Cathedral. Of particular interest are the interior murals, stained glass windows, and the Ghiberti doors. These gilded bronze panels are a reproduction of the famous East Door of the Baptistry in Florence, Italy. The doors are protected by guard rails and are only open on special occasions.

Across from the Cathedral is the Masonic Temple, a spacious auditorium used for fine arts and musical productions. It is open to visitors Monday through Friday from 8:45 A.M. to 4:30 P.M. Of special interest are the heroic carvings on the California Street side of the marble temple and the plastic translucent mural windows.

Telegraph Hill

At Lombard and Kearny streets you pick up the road that climbs up Telegraph Hill to Coit Tower. Parking space at the top of the hill is limited, but with patience you can usually get a place. Or you can leave your car at the garage on the corner of Filbert and Grant and board the Coit bus (number 39) at Stockton and Filbert. It will take you to the top and, if you prefer, you can walk down the footpath on the east slope of the hill.

Telegraph Hill gives a good view of San Francisco's waterfront, Russian Hill, Nob Hill, the Bay and Golden Gate bridges, Alcatraz Island, Angel Island, Treasure Island, and on a clear day some East Bay landmarks.

For an even loftier view, take the elevator (25 cents) to the top of Coit Tower (210 feet high). The elevator operates daily from 11 A.M. to 4:30 P.M. Monday through Friday, 10 A.M. to 5 P.M. Saturday and Sunday.

CYLINDRICAL Coit Tower, rising from atop Telegraph Hill, is famous San Francisco landmark.

Coit Tower, dramatically lit at night, is a well-known landmark against the city skyline. It was built in 1934 as a memorial to the city's volunteer firemen from funds left to the city by Lillie Hitchcock Coit, a great fire buff. The shape of the tower is often said to be that of a fire nozzle. Inside the fluted cylindrical column you will see murals done by artists in 1934 under the Work Projects Administration.

If you choose to walk down from Telegraph Hill, take the pathway that curves down the eastern slope. You will come to two sets of steps, one leading to Filbert and the other to Greenwich. Either stairway takes you down to Montgomery, a short distance below, and then drops down a long steep flight to Sansome at the foot of the hill.

Russian Hill

Located west of Telegraph Hill, roughly between Hyde, Taylor, Vallejo, and Greenwich, is Russian Hill. In the immediate area you will find small green parks, quaint cottages, and skyscraper apartment buildings. Here you can drive on two of San Francisco's most interesting streets. Filbert between Hyde and Leavenworth is one of the city's steepest streets; Lombard between Hyde and Leavenworth is the crookedest—the brick road coils down in snake-like fashion amidst bright hydrangea gardens.

Twin Peaks

Situated in the center of the city, Twin Peaks give the best look at San Francisco, a good look at the East Bay, and on a clear day a glimpse of the Farallon Islands, 30 miles out in the Pacific. To reach the summit, take Upper Market Street to Twin Peaks Boulevard. Follow the Boulevard to the "figure-eight" road which circles the peaks, and stop at the observation area.

THE NORTH WATERFRONT

San Francisco's north waterfront, run-down and neglected a decade ago, is now pulling and pleasing tremendous crowds. Today, this 22-block district fronts on small parks, contains two unusual museums, art galleries, five old ships on public display, many restaurants, excellent shopping, small theaters, good parking, and some good walking.

Here are the turn-around points for two of the city's cable car lines, Beniamino Bufano's much-traveled statue of St. Francis, the pier for the bay tour boats, the city's largest import bazaar, a shopping complex in a former chocolate factory, and another in a refurbished cannery.

For an overall view of the area, ride the double-decker bus, which starts on Beach Street, just west of Larkin. It lumbers east across the district to Fisherman's Wharf, and returns to Beach, stopping on request.

Aquatic Park

The most pleasant way to arrive at the north waterfront is by cable car. The Powell-Hyde Street line reaches its turntable in little Victorian Park. Two blocks west is the Maritime Museum (open daily from 10 A.M. to 5 P.M.) at the foot of Polk Street. Inside the museum is a seafaring exhibit that takes you back to the days when the edge of the bay was a forest of tall masts.

Moored along the Hyde Street Pier just north of the museum are four old ships. The three-masted schooner *C. A. Thayer*, the steam schooner *Wapama*, the ferry boat *Eureka*, and the scow schooner *Alma* are all symbols of the era when wooden vessels were the principal cargo carriers on the coast. Visitors can board all but the *Alma* daily from 10 A.M. to 10 P.M. Admission is 50 cents for adults, 25 cents for children.

Ghirardelli Square

Just south and west of San Francisco's floating maritime museum, covering the block bounded by Beach, Larkin, North Point, and Polk streets, is Ghirardelli Square. First a woolen works and later the Ghirardelli Chocolate Factory, this red-brick building complex has been remodeled and restored to contain a variety of shops, two art galleries, theaters, a radio station, and many restaurants.

Ghirardelli Square includes a number of buildings (with names such as Mustard, Cocoa, and Chocolate), all of which are situated around an inviting plaza. The brick tower that marks Ghirardelli Square was copied from one at the Chateau Blois in France. If you wish to rest, select one of the benches near the splashing fountain or one which affords a view of the bay and boats.

Shops in the Square contain imports from such places as Africa, Holland, Ireland, the Orient, Finland, and Greece. Other stores contain wearing apparel, children's toys, cutlery, flowers, jewelry, and leather goods.

SAN FRANCISCO'S VICTORIANS

Despite the widespread destruction of the 1906 earthquake and fire, many San Francisco Victorian houses are still standing in all their former glory. Characterized by towers, columned porches, wooden filigree, stained glass, and bay windows, many have been restored to preserve their gingerbread charm.

Touring the city, you can find examples of Queen Anne, Stick, Italiante, and Georgian houses that give the feel of another era.

In the Mission District, drive down Guerrero, Dolores, Sanchez, Noe, 20th, 21st, 22nd, and 23rd streets. In Pacific Heights, try Vallejo, Broadway, Jackson, Washington, Pierce, Scott, and Divisadero streets, and Pacific Avenue. Numbers 2229 and 2231 Divisadero Street were remodeled by Julia Morgan, designer of William Randolph Hearst's San Simeon.

On Russian Hill, visit Green and Vallejo streets and Russian Hill Place. West of Van Ness there are good examples on Clay, Sacramento, California, Pine, Bush, Sutter, Post, Laguna, Buchanan, Webster, Steiner, and Baker streets. Note the unusual Vedanta Temple at 2963 Webster Street.

IMAGINATIVE RENOVATIONS have converted old brick structures into Ghirardelli Square (left) and The Cannery (right). Both offer interesting and varied shops, restaurants, views.

Part of Ghirardelli Square's charm lies in the outdoor cafes and in the variety of food available here. For instance, you can watch thin crepes being made, sample some Mexican or Italian food, or enjoy a Twin Peaks sundae or a Golden Gate Banana Split at an old time ice cream parlor. Also at the Ghirardelli Chocolate Manufactory and Fountain you can watch chocolate being made.

If you have your car with you, there is an underground garage. The entrance is on the Beach Street side of the Square, and there is a parking charge.

The Cannery

Similar to Ghirardelli Square in some ways, The Cannery is bounded by Beach, Leavenworth, and Jefferson streets. Originally constructed in 1894 to house the Del Monte Fruit Cannery, the old brick building with its concrete walkways and arched windows has been restored and refurbished.

The Cannery contains three levels of shopping pleasures. You can buy an assortment of goods, from contemporary household furnishings to primitive art objects. Other shops feature such items as candles, flowers, linens, books, and pet supplies.

Outside escalators and stairs provide access to the different floors, or you can take a glass-enclosed elevator from the ground floor to the top. From the third floor you can see Alcatraz Island, the *Balclutha,* (see page 21), the Bay Bridge, and Coit Tower.

On the west side of The Cannery is a plaza containing a small garden center, outside tables, and an oyster bar. Other restaurants in the complex feature Oriental, Mexican, French, or English food.

Across Leavenworth Street from The Cannery is a parking lot which provides one hour free parking with your ticket validated from The Cannery.

Fisherman's Wharf

San Francisco's famous wharf is just several blocks east of The Cannery at Jones and Jefferson. If you are downtown, take the cable car to its Taylor and Bay street turntable.

Jefferson Street is one vast open-air fish market. You will see huge kettles of steaming crabs, and lots of sour dough French bread. A popular item here is a seafood cocktail, which vendors sell in disposable containers. Beyond the fish counters, activity centers around the fishing boats (about 200) as they come in with their catch. At the foot of Jones and Leavenworth streets the boats stop while crates of fish are hoisted to the pier.

THREE-MASTED BALCLUTHA, docked east of Fisherman's Wharf, sailed the seas from 1880's to 1920's.

LIVE CRABS are boiled in steaming cauldrons at many open-air markets lining Fisherman's Wharf.

Balclutha

About two blocks east along the wharf is the permanent berth of the *Balclutha*, a handsome old three-masted sailing ship. Refurbished and restored, she looks like what she was: a Scottish-built, square-rigged ship that plied the seas between the 1880's and the 1920's, and a veteran of 17 Cape Horn crossings. You can go aboard from 9:30 A.M. to 10:30 P.M. daily, inspect the wheel house, the red-plush-upholstered chart house, the captain's cabin, and the ship's galley. Admission is $1 for adults; 50 cents for children 12 to 17; 25 cents for children 6-11.

Boat tours

For striking views of San Francisco from the water, take a sightseeing tour of the bay on one of the trim ships of the Red and White Fleet. They leave from pier 43½ near Fisherman's Wharf. The route will take you close to the Golden Gate Bridge, past the grim rock that was Alcatraz Prison until it was abandoned in 1963, past Treasure Island, under the Bay Bridge, and along the waterfront. From shipboard you see San Francisco and the surrounding area as a dramatic rim around the bay. The city's buildings look higher than ever, and its streets are wide strips

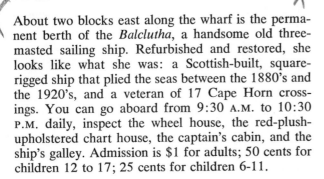

running downhill to the water. To the north lie the gentle hills of Marin County, and to the east Oakland and Berkeley spread out along the shore and up into the hills.

Boats for the 1¼-hour excursions leave frequently between 10 A.M. and 5 P.M. during the summer months, and between 11 A.M. and 4 P.M. during the winter months. The Red and White fleet also offers excursions to Angel Island. It gets chilly on the bay, so take along a wrap and a scarf.

Shopping

In the north waterfront district you will see items from painted seashells and postcards sold near Fisherman's Wharf to bronze turnbuckles at a ship chandler's; from zebra skins in an import shop to a choice of 200 cheeses on sale at The Cannery.

Biggest and most famous retailer is Cost Plus Imports, a rambling bazaar of housewares, antiques, foods, jewelry, and garden supplies. At the east end of the district is the Northpoint Shopping Center. Its street floor has a candy maker, a market, an ice cream parlor, and several restaurants. Up the escalator is Akron, a sort of home-and-housewares supermarket.

At the west end of the district are Ghirardelli Square and The Cannery. Other shopping on the

north waterfront includes several ship chandlers, scattered antique shops, and much curio selling. A majority of all north waterfront shops are open every day of the week.

Wharf restaurants

For thousands who come to the city, a San Francisco visit automatically calls for a meal at Fisherman's Wharf. The view is a big reason to go. If you get a window table, then below you are the bobbing fishing boats. In the distance are the tall orange-red towers of the Golden Gate Bridge, and beyond them the purple Marin hills.

At the seafood restaurants specialties include fresh crab (during the season, early November to middle June or July), cracked and served cold with lemon and mayonnaise; Crab Louis, the classic Wharf salad, served with San Francisco's sour dough bread; abalone; and cioppino, the heroic fish and shellfish stew which you eat with your fingers.

Restaurants elsewhere along the north waterfront are not easily categorized—however, if you're looking for Italian, Japanese, Mexican, or California food, you can find it here.

ALONG THE OCEAN

San Francisco's ocean waterfront offers no swimming because of the dangerous undertow. However, a variety of other recreational activities are available. You can sun or fish from Presidio beaches, golf among cypress trees, visit an art gallery, zoo, or amusement park, or stroll through historic Fort Point.

Presidio

With more than 1400 acres, the Presidio of San Francisco is the largest military reservation in any American city. But to the residents of San Francisco, the Presidio is a very fine and convenient park. They fish from Presidio beaches and piers; stroll along the wall that separates the military reservation's woods from the sunny yards and elegantly bay-windowed exteriors of Presidio Heights residences; and take in the views of the ocean, bay, headlands, and straits of the Golden Gate.

The Presidio is a command center for military activities in the eight Far Western states. Group tours of the post are conducted by the information office's community relations section. It is advisable to reserve space several months in advance; for reservations call 561-3870.

The main gate to the Presidio is on Lombard Street, a short distance west of where U.S. 101 turns northwest toward the Golden Gate Bridge. You are now on the 49-Mile Drive and will pass the new Letterman

HIDDEN COURTYARD off North Point Street is cool, quiet. Antique shops, on two levels, face court.

BEYOND GOLDEN GATE BRIDGE are tall buildings characteristic of San Francisco skyline. Presidio is wooded area on right; Fort Point huddles under southern approach of bridge.

Hospital, white clapboard houses built in 1870, the Officers' Club which dates back to the Spanish era, Pershing Square with its flagpole (the flag is raised and lowered with military ceremony—the 5 P.M. retreat includes bugle and cannon salutes and an honor detail), and San Francisco National Cemetery. A little past the turnoff to Fort Point, the 49-Mile Drive slips under U.S. 101, parallels the cliff's edge near a line of old gun emplacements, passes the memorial to World War II servicemen lost in West Coast waters, and leaves the Presidio near the end of 25th Avenue.

The Presidio also contains park-like wooded areas, especially on the high ground to the south. One of the best lookouts is from Inspiration Point just off Arguello Boulevard. Also on the south side are a playground, private golf course, and Mountain Lake adjoining Mountain Lake Park. The west side of the Presidio contains popular sand beaches.

A Presidio loop trail has been charted that offers hikers the full range of the post's terrain, views, and points of interest. The Historic Trail Guide folder is available at the Military Police office.

Fort Point

Huddling under the southern end of the Golden Gate Bridge and reached from Lincoln Boulevard is historic Fort Point. Here Colonel Juan Bautista de Anza planted a cross in 1776. In 1853 the Americans, on the site of an old Spanish fort, started work on this massive brick, iron, and granite structure built roughly along the lines of Fort Sumter in South Carolina. The fort, which never fired a defensive shot, has been abandoned since 1914.

The fort's most serious adversary is proving to be the weather. Wind-driven salt water and fog have rusted out the iron balustrades and spiral staircases, and have eaten into the mortar. If the Golden Gate Bridge's imaginative chief engineer, Joseph Strauss, had not ordered construction of a special arch over the fort, it would have been torn down to make way for the bridge in the mid-1930's.

The fort is open between 1 and 4 P.M. on Saturday and Sunday, and visitors may roam at will through the old brick quadrangle. There is also a museum.

BUGLER sounds "To the Colors" as Flag drifts down pole to color guard. Public is welcome at Presidio's daily ritual.

FORT POINT, once guardian of bay entrance, is now rusting relic.

Golden Gate Bridge

One of the best things about San Francisco's Golden Gate Bridge is that you can walk across it. As a pedestrian, you can enjoy views that are denied the automobile traveler.

Park your car at the toll plaza, pay 10 cents to get on the bridge, and walk out to the middle and back for some magnificent views of the San Francisco skyline. The Marin County lookout at the north end of the bridge gives an exceptional wide-angle view of the city.

To drive across the Golden Gate Bridge, you pay a 50 cent toll coming into San Francisco. When heading north you do not stop to pay.

Plans are being made to turn the land around the San Francisco end of the bridge into a recreational area which will include an observation post, a bicycle route linking San Francisco and Marin counties, and a small park.

Lincoln Park

El Camino del Mar, an extension of Lincoln Boulevard in the Presidio, takes you to Lincoln Park. Here is a municipal 18-hole golf course, and a fine art gallery, the California Palace of the Legion of Honor.

You will see works by the great masters, a special collection of graphic prints, and Rodin's *Thinker* in the courtyard. The museum is open daily from 10 A.M to 5 P.M.

Land's End

For a look at Mile Rock Lighthouse, the Golden Gate Bridge, and the Pacific Ocean, take the northern turn-off from Point Lobos Avenue to Land's End. Besides a view, you'll see the shelled bridge of the *USS San Francisco*, torpedoed in 1942 at Guadalcanal.

San Francisco Zoological Gardens

Adults as well as youngsters will enjoy a visit to San Francisco's fine zoo. It's out at the edge of Ocean Beach (turn off the Great Highway at either Sloat Boulevard or Park Road) and is open every day from 10 A.M to 5:30 P.M. You can easily walk around the zoo, where you can look through the fences at animals roaming in surroundings similar to their natural habitat. Or you can take the motor-drawn "Elephant Train" which circles the entire zoo. Three strings of open cars leave every half hour from the Giraffe Barn near the main entrance and take adults and children on a 20-minute circuit.

Behind the zoo is Fleishhacker Pool, one of the world's longest. The pool, which holds six million gallons of warmed seawater, is open from 10 A.M. to 5 P.M. April to November.

Next to the zoo, the San Francisco Recreation and Park Department presents Storyland, a child's wonderland of well-known story book characters. Permanent exhibits include Rapunzel's Castle, the Gingerbread House, Cinderella's Coach, and the Old Lady's Shoe House. There is also a prairie dog village and a lake and moats for water birds. Storyland is open from 10 A.M to 5:30 P.M. from March 15 through December. It is closed on Mondays and Tuesdays except during the summer season (mid-June to early September) when it remains open seven days a week.

GOLDEN GATE PARK

San Francisco owes a great debt of gratitude to the late John McLaren whose vision and perseverance in San Francisco's early days turned more than 1,000 acres of rolling sand dunes into a park. Today Golden Gate Park is one of the really great metropolitan parks of the world.

Park visitors benefit from an enlightened policy of operation: the park is meant to be used. You can park your car along most of the drives—on Sunday auto traffic is restricted along sections of John F. Kennedy Drive—there are few "No Parking" signs. You can walk, play, or picnic on the grass anywhere except the small plot of lawn surrounding Mr. McLaren's statue in Rhododendron Dell. The bridle paths, equestrian field, and bicycle trails are for public use; you can rent horses at the stables near Kennedy Drive (Main Drive) and Spreckels Lake.

The Museum and Academy of Science buildings, the concessions, the Arboretum, and the Conservatory close at night; otherwise the park is open from dawn until 10 P.M.

Along John F. Kennedy Drive

If you enter the park at its northwest corner, you will enter on John F. Kennedy Drive. On the left side of the road is a Dutch windmill; on the other side is Arctic explorer Roald Amundsen's Norwegian sloop *Gjoa*, the first ship to navigate the Northwest Passage. Visitors are not allowed to board the ship.

The nine-hole pitch-and-putt golf course a short distance inside the park is open every day. To get to the clubhouse, turn left at the first intersection of Kennedy Drive after you leave the Great Highway.

The Chain of Lakes, a series of three artificial lakes, runs from north to south across the park near its western end. Largest of the three is North Lake, north of Kennedy Drive. It is dotted with several landscaped islands. The banks of Middle Lake, south of Kennedy Drive, are planted with camellias and Japanese cherry trees, while South Lake, smallest in the chain, hosts large numbers of wild ducks.

North of Kennedy Drive, just east of the Chain of Lakes, the fences of the Buffalo Paddock are carefully concealed by artful landscaping so that buffalo and elk within the enclosure seem to be roaming at large.

Anglers will find an ideal practicing spot at the Flycasting Pool south of Kennedy Drive. The cement-lined pool is divided into three sections—one for distance casting, one for accuracy, and a third for practicing difficult overhead casts.

As you approach Spreckels Lake, you will pass some of the largest and oldest rhododendrons in the park. They are planted on an island in the center of Kennedy Drive and are at their best in May.

The lake itself is to the north of the drive. Its waters are usually dotted with wildfowl, and during the summer the lake is used for sailing model boats. The San Francisco Model Yacht Club has its headquarters in the building just to the west of the lake.

Polo matches are frequently held on Sunday from April to October in Golden Gate Park Polo Fields located just east of the Flycasting Pool.

Continuing east on Kennedy Drive, you pass 25-acre Lindley Meadow and tiny Lloyd Lake. A gravel path encircles the lake, leading to the "Portals of the Past" on its shore. The six white marble pillars that form the portals were the entrance to the A. N. Towne

SUNSET MAGAZINE Demonstration Gardens, at Strybing Arboretum, offer ideas for home landscaping.

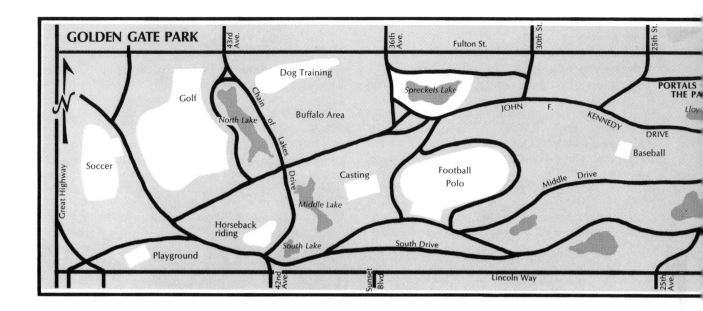

residence on Nob Hill. They were all that remained of the house after the 1906 fire, and Mrs. Towne later presented them to the park.

Stow Lake is the largest of the park's man-made lakes. It is the central reservoir for the park's irrigation system and is also a popular recreation spot. There is a snack bar near the dock where boats can be rented. Tree-lined walks border the lake, and a road goes around it. Two bridges lead to Strawberry Hill, a wooded island in the center of the lake. A five-minute walk up a fairly stiff slope puts you on top of the hill. From the summit you see the park as a wide green swath through the west end of the city, the towers of the Golden Gate and Bay bridges, the surf pounding the shoreline, and on clear days, the Farallon Islands, 30 miles out into the Pacific.

Just east of the Stow Lake Drive on the north side of Kennedy Drive, the Rose Garden contains about seventy-five varieties of roses, including recent award winners. All are labeled.

The M. H. de Young Museum

On the west side of the Music Concourse is the M. H. de Young Memorial Museum, opened in 1895 after Michael de Young, publisher of the San Francisco *Chronicle*, proposed that the profits of the California Midwinter International Exposition of 1894 be used to house a permanent collection of art. The original museum buildings were torn down in 1926 and today's museum consists of two wings extending from either side of a 134-foot tower facing a landscaped court. The Pool of Enchantment at the entrance is the work of sculptor M. Earl Cummings as is the bronze

Sun Dial at the building's southeast corner.

A special wing overlooking the Japanese Tea Garden was added in 1966 to house the Avery Brundage Collection of Oriental Art. On display are nearly 6,000 treasures covering 60 centuries of Asian civilization.

The museum houses extensive and varied art collections displayed in spacious galleries enclosing the court. Paintings include works by famous American and European artists. Its doors are open daily from 10 A.M. to 5 P.M.

Japanese Tea Garden

The Tea Garden just west of the museum is open daily from 8 A.M. to dusk. Here, in addition to interesting plantings, you will find a moon bridge, a temple, Oriental gateways and lanterns, a large bronze Buddha, and a tea house where you can get green or jasmine tea and Oriental cookies served by Japanese girls. The garden is planted with camellias, magnolia trees, red-leafed Japanese maples, and miniature trees. In spring, the cherry trees make the garden a fairyland of delicate blooms. Blossoms are at their peak around April 1.

The Academy of Sciences

The California Academy of Sciences grouping includes the North American Hall with its collection of American mammals and birds displayed in their natural habitats; the African Hall, which features an African water hole with specimens of giraffes, gnus, impalas, gazelles, zebras, and hartebeests grouped

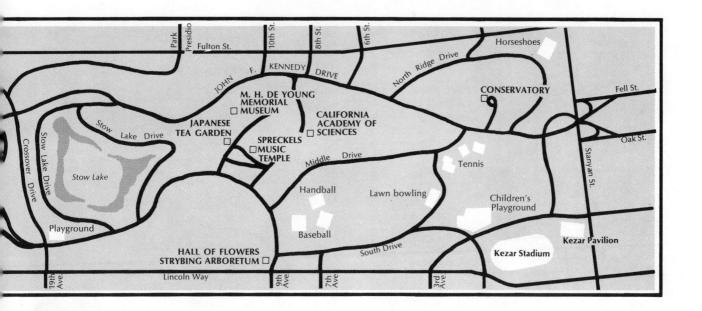

around it; the Steinhart Aquarium, a most popular attraction; and the Morrison Planetarium.

The Academy of Sciences and the Aquarium are open every day from 10 A.M. to 5 P.M.; admission is free. The Planetarium has at least three shows daily during the summer and at least one show in the winter. Evening shows are presented 5 nights a week. Admission is $1 for adults, 50 cents for children under 16.

Music Concourse

Situated between the de Young Museum and the Academy of Sciences is the Music Concourse where people gather on Sundays and holidays (weather permitting) at 2 P.M. for a band concert. You can sit on the terraces around the Concourse or on benches.

The Strybing Arboretum

A stroll through the Arboretum is a "must" for anyone interested in plants. Here in this self-contained, 60-acre world are about 5,000 species and varieties of plants from all over the globe conveniently arranged according to geographical origin and carefully labeled.

Of particular interest are the *Sunset Magazine* Demonstration Home Gardens, designed to help home owners with ideas for plant selection and planting design as well as for landscape construction.

The Arboretum is located along South Drive and is open from 8 A.M. to 4:30 P.M. on weekdays and from 10 A.M. to 5 P.M. on Saturday and Sunday. Admission is free.

Rhododendron Dell

As you leave the museum area and continue east on Kennedy Drive, you come to the John McLaren Memorial Rhododendron Dell. Peak blooming period is early May, but the extensive collection boasts something of interest from February to June.

Fern Dell

Adjacent to Rhododendron Dell to the east is the Tree Fern Forest. The original tree ferns were shipped from Australia some fifty or sixty years ago. Many of them still thrive.

The Conservatory

When you enter the doors of the conservatory (open 8 A.M to 4:50 P.M. daily), you enter another world, where the atmosphere is warm and humid, the plants lush and tropical.

The conservatory houses many fascinating plant collections—brightly colored crotons, large-flowered hibiscus, rare cycads, graceful ferns, orchids. Along the path, among tall palms, are some of the largest and oldest philodendron plants under cultivation.

Be sure to look at the greenhouse itself before you leave. A replica of the conservatory at Kew Gardens, England, it was bought by James Lick, a San Francisco philanthropist, and its sections were brought around the Horn on a sailing ship. After the owner's death, the greenhouse was purchased by the city of San Francisco and erected in Golden Gate Park in 1878. The framework is wood, but unlike most green-

M. H. DE YOUNG MUSEUM, across Music Concourse, has exceptional collection of Oriental art.

STOW LAKE has dock where boats can be rented. You can walk around lake on tree-lined path.

houses, the beams are laminated. If you look closely, you can see how short pieces have been fitted together to form the dome.

In the Conservatory Valley between Kennedy Drive and the conservatory are many formal beds of annuals and bulbs. On the slopes behind these beds are two floral features: a floral design which honors events of national or area importance in living plants; and a floral clock presented to the city by the watchmakers of Switzerland.

Children's Playground

The southeast corner of the park is devoted to recreation, and a principal attraction is the Children's Playground adjacent to the Sharon Building. Neighborhood mothers bring their offspring here during the week, and sightseers visiting the park find that an hour or so of recreation gives youngsters a needed diversion. There is also a small animal farm.

Kezar Stadium

A municipal stadium, Kezar is used principally by local high school football teams. Through 1970 Kezar was the home of San Francisco's professional football team, the 49'ers. Kezar Pavilion, the indoor stadium, is used for sporting events, including professional boxing and roller derby.

OTHER PLACES TO EXPLORE

San Francisco offers other places to explore—you can window shop at a merchandising center, take a look at San Francisco's Italian and Japanese communities, browse through specialty shops on Union Street, or drive by some of San Francisco's most elegant homes.

Jackson Square

Although Jackson Square's showrooms are closed to the general public (except for once a year usually in October), anyone with an enthusiasm for elegant old buildings, or anyone who simply enjoys window shopping, will find a stroll through the Jackson Square area rewarding.

This unique merchandising center supplies Bay Area decorators, architects, and retail outlets with interior furnishings and accessories. The wholesale houses occupy handsomely restored buildings in the area that surrounds Jackson Street—roughly bounded by Montgomery, Washington, and Battery streets, and Pacific Avenue.

Once San Francisco's Barbary Coast, this part of the city became a dismal warehouse area when the city rebuilt in other directions following the 1906 fire. The old buildings were eventually boarded up and deserted and remained so until, in 1951, an enterprising group pioneered the development of the ex-

FIREMEN statue is in Washington Square. Behind: Sts. Peter, Paul Church.

JACKSON SQUARE, once part of Barbary Coast, is lined with restored brick-fronted buildings containing wholesale decorator showrooms.

clusive and unusual decorative center that is today's Jackson Square.

The restored buildings include such old structures as the A. P. Hotaling Co. liquor warehouse, now the Kneedler-Fauchere Building which houses four wholesale fabric showrooms. Around the corner, the McGuire Company has restored the old Hotaling livery stable. Oldest of the area's buildings is 472 Jackson Street; it was the Lucas, Turner & Co. Bank, established in 1853 by General William T. Sherman.

North Beach

Not really a beach at all, the area was so named in the 1850's when North Beach was a protected inlet between Telegraph and Russian hills.

Here, in the center of the Italian community, are Italian bakeries, pastry shops, delicatessens, and kitchen specialty stores. In the pastry shops you'll find rum babas, marzipan, and cylindrical *cannolis* filled with sweetened ricotta cheese and glaceed fruits.

The bakeries, or bread shops, offer long loaves of sweet and sour dough French breads and *panettone,* a round Italian sweet bread filled with raisins and candied fruits.

The kitchen specialty shops sell noodle machines, cheese graters, *caffe espresso* machines, ravioli rolling sticks, baking irons for *pizzele* and *cialdi* cookies, copper *polenta pots*, and round-bottomed pans.

Excellent meals are served in the restaurants of North Beach. Besides the well-known establishments, there are modest, unassuming little ones that serve savory specialties. Also within the North Beach area are a number of lively night spots featuring jazz combos, comedians, and dancers.

Columbus Avenue cuts right across the North Beach area, and at Columbus and Union is Washington Square, a small, very green park. The Church of Saints Peter and Paul is across Filbert Street from the Square. Its two tall towers, illuminated at night, are visible from many sections of the city.

For many years, a flourishing colony of painters, writers, and craftsmen have had their headquarters within North Beach. Once a year, usually in June, they display their crafts in a street bazaar that draws thousands of art lovers to look or to buy. To inspect this interesting area, walk north on Grant Avenue beyond Columbus. You'll pass small galleries, studios, and shops, some brightly painted outposts of the city's bohemian life. Inside are ceramics, paintings, jewelry, poster art, cloth dolls, and sandals.

Interspersed along Grant and adjacent streets are meat markets, espresso houses, bakeries, and a ravioli factory.

Parking in the district is at a premium at all times. But the Taylor and Bay cable car runs along Mason between Vallejo and Union, and from there it's only a three-block walk east to the shops on Grant Avenue.

TURN-OF-THE-CENTURY flavor is preserved along Union Street. Victorian and old-frame dwellings have been converted into specialty shops, decorator showrooms, galleries, restaurants.

Pacific Heights

Along Pacific Avenue (and Broadway, Jackson, and Washington), west of Van Ness Avenue, are some of San Francisco's most elegant dwellings. With formal, tailored entry gardens, they are sophisticated town houses in the European manner. Recently many modern skyscraper apartments have been added in the area.

A slow drive up and down Pacific and Broadway also is worthwhile just for the superb view, for these streets hug the crest of the ridge called Pacific Heights, with the Marina, the Golden Gate, and Marin County spread out beyond.

Dwellings of particular interest are: the California Historical Society's headquarters at 2090 Jackson Street, built in the Victorian style in 1896, and the Spreckels mansion at 2080 Washington.

Union Street

Once a pasture for dairy herds, Union Street from the 1700 to 2200 blocks is now a fashionable shopping sector with a charming turn-of-the-century flavor. You can take public transportation to Union Street (call Municipal Railway Information Service for which bus line to take) or if you choose to drive, the intersecting side streets offer parking.

Union Street is best explored on foot. There are home furnishing stores, decorator showrooms, art galleries, antique and import shops, florists, book stores, custom clothiers, and a variety of restaurants including Creole, Mexican, and Japanese. There is also an auction gallery.

Of historical interest is the Octagon House at the corner of Gough and Union streets. Built in 1857, the house has been completely restored and is open to the public the first Sunday and second and fourth Thursdays of every month from 1 to 4 P.M.

Japanese Cultural and Trade Center

Until recently San Francisco's Japantown, the small area spreading out from the intersection of Post and Buchanan streets, had no highly conspicuous landmark to flag your attention. A district of big, faded, Victorian-style houses and small shops where many of the city's 12,000 Japanese-Americans live, it attracted few visitors.

But that has changed with the opening of the Japanese Cultural and Trade Center. A string of handsome white buildings between Geary Expressway and Post Street, the center starts on the east at Laguna Street past Buchanan, boldly leaps Webster Street with a curved bridgeway of shops, and ends on the west at Fillmore Street. Tenants include the

Japanese Consulate, manufacturers with showrooms for industrial equipment, and retailers selling goods ranging from bonsai plants to pearls. Occasionally demonstrations of Japanese painting are given.

In the complex are three commercial buildings, a 14-story hotel of Japanese decor, a theater, and restaurants. A garage (main entrance is on Geary) can accommodate 800 cars. There is also a spacious Peace Plaza containing a five-tiered 35-foot Peace Pagoda in the center of a reflecting pool. Showrooms are open daily from 9 A.M. to 5 P.M., stores from 10 A.M. to 6 or 8 P.M.

ENTERTAINMENT AND CULTURAL ACTIVITIES

San Francisco is a theater city. The downtown houses (the Curran and the Geary) play Broadway musicals, comedies, and dramas more or less continuously. The Geary and the Marines' Memorial Theatre (Sutter and Mason streets) host the popular American Conservatory Theatre productions. For information concerning their season write to A.C.T., 450 Geary, San Francisco, 94102 or call 771-3880.

Several workshops and little theaters (especially at North Beach and the north waterfront) offer both Broadway and experimental productions. San Francisco newspapers carry complete listings, or dial 391-2000 for a recorded summary of the day's events.

San Francisco has the largest permanent opera in the West. The season opens in mid-September and continues for about eleven weeks.

The symphony season starts early in December and continues until mid-May. Concerts and ballets of civic as well as visiting companies appear at the Opera House and Masonic Auditorium at various times during the year.

On the more informal side, Sigmund Stern Grove at 19th Avenue and Sloat Boulevard offers outdoor concerts on Sundays during the summer. For information on their program write to the San Francisco Recreation and Park Department.

Art Galleries

San Franciscans support three major art museums with frequent changes of exhibitions and occasional traveling shows, in addition to their permanent collections. These galleries are The California Palace of the Legion of Honor in Lincoln Park; the M. H. de Young Memorial Museum in Golden Gate Park; and the San Francisco Museum of Art at the Veterans Building in Civic Center.

In addition to the three art museums, there are countless small galleries throughout the city and frequent outdoor art shows. Check the local newspapers for current exhibits.

PEACE PAGODA, at center of Japanese Cultural and Trade Center, is a nighttime landmark.

THE EAST BAY

Oakland • University of California • Mount Diablo

Campanile, Berkeley campus

Crowded into a narrow strip between the water of San Francisco Bay and the low hills that rise to the east, the East Bay communities parallel the shoreline, flowing into one another so that you scarcely know when you depart one and enter the next.

Four bridges stretch across San Francisco Bay to the East Bay Communities. They are, from north to south, Richmond-San Rafael Bridge, San Francisco-Oakland Bay Bridge, San Mateo Bridge, and Dumbarton Bridge.

Although the East Bay's "big city" reputation may not equal that of San Francisco's, some of its attractions can match or even exceed those of the fabled sister in whose shadow Oakland and its surrounding towns dwell.

OAKLAND

The major East Bay city and the second largest city in Northern California, Oakland is an important industrial center and shipping port. Long in the background of San Francisco, Oakland has emerged finally as a city in its own right. In addition to several recreational areas, Oakland has an international airport, an impressive sports complex, and an exceptional new museum.

For an overall view of the Oakland area (including the nearby cities of Alameda, Piedmont, and Berkeley), take a summer sightseeing bus tour. On the two-and-a-half hour tour, which operates between Memorial Day and Labor Day, guides narrate historical features of the area. The tour begins at Jack London Square daily except Monday at 1 P.M.

If you wish to explore the area by car yourself, follow the bright blue "Scenic Tour Oakland" signs, starting with Jack London Square.

For more specific tour information, write to the Oakland Chamber of Commerce Convention and Tourism Bureau, 1320 Webster Street, Oakland, California 94612.

Lake Merritt's North Shore

A favorite recreational spot for Oakland and other East Bay residents, Lake Merritt is a 155-acre body of salt water right in the heart of the city. The Y-shaped lake is encircled by a park strip and a main thoroughfare. Green lawns and cool shade greet you as you turn off Grand Avenue and enter Lakeside Park which offers a variety of activities.

Children's Fairyland, a land of make-believe, is a collection of "sets," replicas of settings of favorite

Countryside near Mt. Diablo

Lake Merritt, a quiet retreat close to downtown Oakland

nursery rhymes. To enter you step (adults stoop) through the "instep" in the dwelling of the Old Woman Who Lived in a Shoe.

Paths through the landscaped grounds lead you to such other sets as the Sugar Plum Tree, Three Men in a Tub, the Walrus and the Carpenter, Chinese Tree House, and the Owl and the Pussycat. When appropriate, the sets are animated with live pets that children may feed—like Mary's lamb, monkeys in Noah's Ark, the Little Red Hen, and cavorting sea lions outside the house of the carpenter.

Fairyland is open from 10 A.M. to 5:30 P.M. daily during the summer months; Wednesday through Sunday in spring and fall; Saturday, Sunday, and holidays during the winter.

The Lakeside Nursery Gardens, just east of Fairyland, serve as a propagating nursery for the plants, shrubs, and trees that are planted in the Oakland parks and as a year-round show garden of colorful flower displays. In the heart of the gardens is the Lakeside Park Garden Center building where garden club meetings and flower shows are held. An authentic Japanese Garden is situated outside the Center building with trial and show gardens located south of the building. All gardens as well as a lathhouse-greenhouse complex are open to the public.

An area on the northeast arm of the lake is the oldest waterfowl refuge in the country. It was set aside in 1870 for the protection of the ducks and other waterfowl that flock to the lake. Between November and April, the bird count here sometimes goes as high as 5,000.

You can buy a bag of grain and feed the birds yourself, or watch them any day at 3:30 P.M. being fed by park naturalists. Also at 3:30 P.M. is a talk which helps you identify the migratory birds currently occupying the refuge. Some of the birds usually in residence are the Whistling Swan (only wild swan in California), Coot (or mud hen), Pintail, Mallard, and Canvasback. Birds banded here have been traced as far away as Siberia.

Adjacent to the duck feeding area is the Rotary Natural Science Center. Open daily from 10 A.M. to 5 P.M., its handsome and informative exhibits appeal to both amateur and professional natural scientists.

The sailboat clubhouse near the wildlife refuge has launching facilities for sailboats or motor boats. Indoor storage areas for sailboats are also available here for a small fee. On the west shore of Lake Merritt is the main boathouse where you can rent canoes, rowboats, and sailboats. Launch trips around the lake leave from here at frequent intervals during the day.

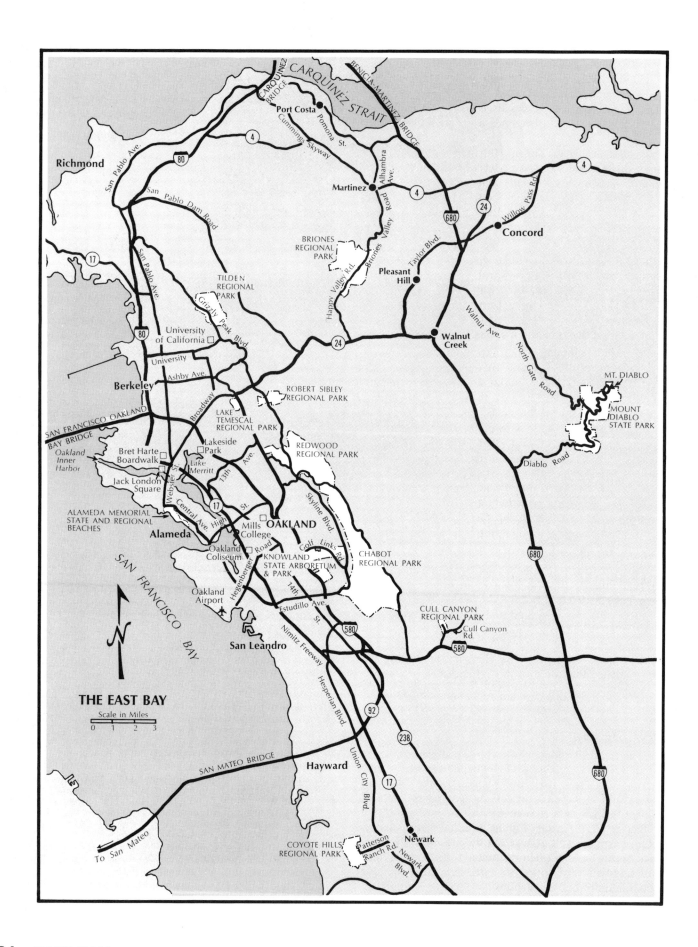

THE EAST BAY

Scale in Miles

0 1 2 3

Oakland Museum

Oakland's exciting new museum covers four square blocks and sits alongside and beneath an evergreen park. The three-tiered complex is so constructed that the roof of each level becomes a garden and terrace for the one above.

To enter the museum at 10th and Fallon streets, on the south shore of Lake Merritt, you walk down, not up. The interior is quiet and cool and the passageway to the grassy inner courtyard is dimly lit. Trees and the wall around the park help to mute traffic noises and block out the architectural jumble of surrounding buildings.

The roof terraces look like giant steps, each row neatly topped with trees or shrubs. From the higher terraces you can see the blue water of Lake Merritt. Beneath you are the three principal gallery levels. Glass doors line the garden side of each level and offer ready exits to outdoor areas.

On the first level are the natural sciences in the Hall of California Ecology. In eight environmental zones, the viewer learns about California's climate, wildlife, and natural features through photographs and skillfully executed dioramas.

Walkways lead up to Cowell Hall of California History on the second level (there is, also, an inside elevator). Two of the items on display are a meticulously restored American-La France fire engine that was used in the 1906 San Francisco disaster and a shiny black Brewster brougham carriage.

The third floor houses the Gallery of California Art, including paintings, sculptures, graphics, prints, illustrations, photographs, and crafts. For work to be eligible for the exhibit, the subject must be Californian or the artist must have resided in the state. The oldest item here, an engraving that shows Sir Francis Drake greeting the assembled Indians on his arrival in California, was drawn in 1599.

Museum hours are 10 A.M. to 5 P.M. Tuesday through Thursday, Saturday and Sunday; 10 A.M. to 10 P.M. Friday. Admission is free. In addition to streetside parking nearby, there is space for nearly 200 cars beneath the museum.

Kaiser Center

The 28-story Kaiser Center, home of Kaiser Industries, covers the block bounded by Lakeside Drive, 20th, Webster, and 21st streets. Of particular interest is an attractive roof garden atop the center's garage.

The garden is remarkable because all of the plants grow in artificial soil. Altogether there are some 5,000 cubic yards of this planting mix on the roof of the garage. In it are planted 42 specimen trees, 1,700 shrubs, and hundreds of flowers. The landscaping is completed by a lawn, a pool with 8,800 square feet

OAKLAND MUSEUM roof garden is terraced, open to gallery levels, linked by stairway to courtyard below.

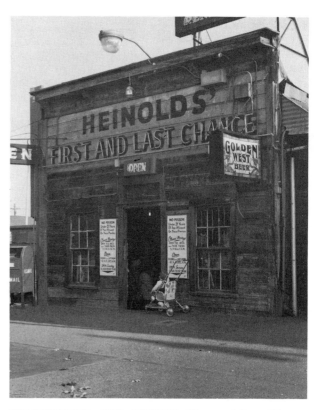

EUCALYPTUS line pathway along Kapiolani Road on the Mills campus, a women's college in Oakland.

WEATHERED AND RUSTIC, First and Last Chance Saloon in Oakland was frequented by Jack London.

of water surface, and three fountains. A restaurant offering French cuisine overlooks the garden.

Jack London Square

Oakland's waterfront, the birthplace of the city, centers around historic Jack London Square, a ten-block area located on the Oakland Estuary at the foot of Broadway. Here, around landscaped malls, shipping wharves, and marina docks, are some of Oakland's finest restaurants and shops.

Of special interest is the First and Last Chance Saloon, a weathered and rustic old building located on the edge of the Square at 50 Webster Street. Built in 1880 from the remains of an old whaling ship, the building was first a bunkhouse for oystermen and later a saloon. A favorite hangout of California author Jack London as a boy, the saloon is filled with photos and mementoes of London. The saloon is open from 1 P.M. to 2 A.M. daily except Sunday.

Bret Harte Boardwalk

Close to Jack London Square, at Fifth Street between Jefferson and Clay, is Bret Harte Boardwalk. Visitors can browse along the one-block array of old Victorian houses and barns which have been renovated

and turned into unique specialty shops, tearooms, and restaurants. The Boardwalk is dedicated to Francis Bret Harte, the famed Western author of the late 19th century, whose house used to stand across the street from the boardwalk where the present freeway is.

Knowland Arboretum and State Park

Animals—real ones and sculptured ones—welcome visitors to the Oakland Zoo, located at Knowland State Park. One observation point allows you to look a Bengal tiger right in the eye. From across a narrow moat, you can toss peanuts to Malaysian sun bears. Children are welcome to pick up the goat kids and piglets, and to pet a baby llama.

A unique ape cage, 50 feet high, dramatically towers over the park like a giant inverted basket. For a good look at the entire zoo, there is a child-scaled train which makes regular trips through the zoo.

Zoo hours are 9 A.M. to 4:30 P.M. Monday through Friday, 9 A.M. to 5:30 P.M. Saturday and Sunday.

At the Knowland Arboretum, you'll see plants and trees (especially oaks) from all over the world.

To reach the park, take the Golf Links Road turnoff from MacArthur Freeway (Interstate 580).

OAKLAND'S COLISEUM complex contains an indoor arena and an outdoor stadium. Besides hosting spectator sports, the complex is used for exhibitions, stage shows, and civic and cultural activities.

Harrison Railroad Park

You'll see some fine examples of Western railroad history at Harrison Railroad Park, at the corner of Harrison and Seventh streets. Four railroad vehicles are placed on a pleasant green lawn shaded by some of Oakland's biggest and oldest trees. The locomotive, day coach, and superintendent's car are open to the public from 10 A.M. to 4 P.M. Wednesday through Sunday.

Mills College

Almost totally surrounded by wooded hills, the 150-acre campus of Mills College can hardly be seen from the road. Once inside the gates of this highly-regarded liberal arts college for women, you'll see eucalyptus-lined walkways, footbridges over Leona Creek, Lake Aliso, and a variety of buildings which house the workings of the college.

Mills has occupied this park-like setting since 1871 when the college moved from Benicia to Oakland. The Victorian-style Mills Hall, the oldest building on campus, dates back to 1873. This administration building, formerly a residence hall, stands across the Oval from the Campanile. The bell tower, of Spanish design, chimes the quarter hour with ten bells cast in 1893.

Most of the buildings on the campus are of traditional Spanish design; however, many new buildings have been added in a contemporary Spanish style. Of particular interest is the octagonal redwood chapel where services are conducted in the round.

To reach Mills College, take the MacArthur Boulevard exit off the MacArthur Freeway (Interstate 580) and enter through Richards Gate, the main entrance. Visitors are welcome the year around. For conducted tour information, write to Public Information, Mills College, Oakland, California 94613.

Oakland sports complex

The Oakland-Alameda County Coliseum complex is two separate circular structures—an outdoor stadium and an indoor arena. At the outdoor stadium you can watch professional football and baseball, while at the arena are ice hockey, basketball, stage shows, and civic and cultural activities. The Coliseum complex is well-designed—every seat is comfortable and provides a good view of the attraction. Adjacent to the arena floor is an Exhibit Hall where trade, boat, home, and car shows are held.

The Coliseum is just east of the Nimitz Freeway. Take the Hegenberger exit to the spacious parking lot.

SPROUL PLAZA, between Student Union and Sproul Hall, is center of activity at University of California.

UNIVERSITY OF CALIFORNIA

Spreading up into the hills and surrounded by sections of Berkeley, the buildings of the 720-acre Berkeley campus of the University of California stand out against the landscape, with the unmistakable outline of Sather Tower (the Campanile) reaching into the sky above them.

You can spend a pleasant hour or more strolling around the beautifully landscaped campus. Try a picnic lunch in Faculty Glade, or on the tree-shaded lawns behind the Life Sciences Building, or on the benches in the shade of the Campanile.

Parking on the campus is subject to control at all hours. Cars without parking permits are admitted to the campus only after 8 P.M. daily. The campus is always open to public foot traffic. Public parking for limited periods of time is available on the street, and there are parking lots in the business district to the south of the campus. The visitor to Berkeley should be forewarned, however, that parking on the outskirts of the campus is often hard to find.

You will want to see the California Memorial Stadium (it has a seating capacity of 78,000) where the Golden Bear football team plays out its fall schedule; pace across the 133-foot stage of the Greek Theatre, a beautiful amphitheater presented to the university by Phoebe Apperson Hearst in 1903; linger on the footbridges that cross Strawberry Creek, a thin stream that becomes a fairly boisterous one after the first rains; visit the Botanical Garden (located near the stadium in Strawberry Canyon), a 35-acre tract of plantings including many rare rhododendrons, cactus, and succulents.

For a magnificent view of the campus, the whole East Bay area, and San Francisco across the water, take the elevator to the top of the 307-foot Campanile. The tower is open daily from 10 A.M. to 5 P.M. Last trip of the day is at 4:40 P.M.

Two specialized collections that are open to the public are the Museum of Paleontology in the Earth Sciences Building and the Lowie Museum of Anthropology in Kroeber Hall. The Museum of Paleontology contains the largest paleontological collection on the Pacific Coast.

There are always interesting exhibits in the first and second floor lobbies of the Doe Memorial Library. With over 3 million volumes, this library is the largest in the West. It is open from 8 A.M. to 10 P.M. Monday through Friday; 9 A.M. to 5 P.M. Saturday; 1 P.M. to 10 P.M. Sunday.

The University's Bancroft Library contains manuscripts, printed books, maps, pictures, and microfilm pertaining to the history of the American West. On display is Sir Francis Drake's crudely shaped "Plate of Brass." The library is open daily with afternoon hours only on Sunday.

CULL CANYON, one of the East Bay Regional Parks, has a sparkling lagoon and a sandy beach for swimming and sunning. Park also has hiking and riding trails, a lake for boating and fishing.

Visitors to Berkeley can take a walking tour of the campus. The tour begins at the visitors' desk in the Student Union, at the end of Telegraph Avenue, where you pick up a brochure that outlines the nearly two-mile walk (about 1½ hours). The brochure also suggests enough other side trips to fill up an entire day.

Escorted tours leave from the Student Union at 1 P.M. weekdays.

EAST BAY REGIONAL PARKS

In the low hills that rise behind the East Bay cities, some 22,000 acres of beautiful countryside have been set aside for recreational use. About 1,000 acres of San Francisco Bay beach and swampland have also been incorporated by the East Bay Regional Park system, operated by Contra Costa and Alameda counties. Some of the parks are small, some large; some highly developed and some relatively untouched and primitive. Many miles of hiking and bridle trails lead through unspoiled woods and fields, and there are hundreds of spots for picnicking. Swimming, fishing, boating, and archery are offered at most of the parks, which are primarily designed for daytime use. With the exception of Scout camps, camping facilities are not provided.

Parks of particular interest are Charles Lee Tilden Regional Park (botanical gardens, model railway, Little Farm), Lake Temescal Regional Park (a unique entrance tunnel which features brightly-painted walls with interesting art designs), Redwood Regional Park (redwood groves, heated outdoor swimming pool), Anthony Chabot Regional Park (sightseeing tour of lake), Alameda Memorial State and Regional Beaches (beachcombing), and Coyote Hills Regional Park (ancient Indian shellmounds and the Biological Sonar Laboratory).

For detailed information and a free brochure on all the parks in the region, write to the East Bay Regional Park District, 11500 Skyline Boulevard, Oakland, California 94619.

MOUNT DIABLO, in background, affords sweeping views and occasionally gets a coating of winter snow.

RANGER answers visitors' questions after a guided tour of conservationist John Muir's house in Martinez.

MOUNT DIABLO

Mount Diablo's summit is an exceptionally fine place for a view. On a clear day you can see as far as the Sierra, Mount Lassen, San Francisco, and the inland waterways of the Central Valley. Because such an expanse of California can be seen from here, Mount Diablo has been the surveying point for Northern and Central California since 1851.

The best time to visit Mount Diablo is after rain and a strong north wind, although a visit is worth-while even on a foggy day—more common in winter —when ground fog blankets the valley leaving you standing above with the mountain tops.

Mount Diablo's main peak is only 3,849 feet in elevation; however, it seems higher because it rises so abruptly. Occasionally during the winter the coni-cal peak gets a coating of snow.

A state park covers a portion of the area, and facili-ties include 80 campsites, 5 group campsites, and 255 picnicking sites. The park also offers a number of good hiking trails. Gates open at 8 A.M. and close at 8 P.M. except during the winter months when they close at 6 P.M. Entrance fee to the state park is 75 cents per car for day use, $2 per car for overnight camping.

You can reach Mount Diablo from Interstate 680. At Danville take Diablo Road to Black Hawk Road, to South Gate Road which goes to the summit.

A drive on several side roads will show you the north and east side of the mountain and remnants from coal mining days. Morgan Territory Road, a paved but lightly-traveled road, winds for 15 miles along spring-fed streams and beside moss-covered trees. Marsh Creek Road takes you where the slopes of Mount Diablo are quite precipitous and the con-tours sharp and craggy. This road will take you to Clayton, once the place of California's largest coal mining boom and now a small farming town.

Along the Nortonville and Somersville roads you will see a few signs of coal mining sites scattered about the hillsides. The Somersville Cemetery starkly chronicles the lives of the Welsh miners and their families who came to live and work in the hills.

ALONG THE CARQUINEZ STRAIT

Port Costa, seen from the Carquinez Strait, is just a tuck in the rolling Contra Costa hills. Yet this town of 250 residents was in the last part of the 19th century a large wheat shipping port.

To reach Port Costa, take Interstate Highway 80 to Crockett. Turn east at Crockett onto Pomona Street and wind through green hills overlooking the busy strait for three miles. Port Costa's most interesting structures are the empty hotel, the old Chinese laundry, the warehouse-shops, and the charred stumps that mark the site of the docks. All are on Main Street close to the water.

At Martinez, just east of Port Costa is the John Muir Historic Site. You can follow Pomona Street from Port Costa or take Interstate Highway 80 to State Highway 4. Follow Highway 4 to Alhambra Avenue and turn left under the overpass. The John Muir home is about 100 yards beyond the overpass to the left.

The site is dominated by the old, gray, 17-room house in which Muir, ardent conservationist and founder of the Sierra Club, and his wife lived between 1890 and 1914. The rooms are decorated with furniture, clothing, and memorabilia of the period. In the kitchen are the original stove and cooking utensils, and in Muir's study are his desk, samples of his work, and some of his personal effects.

Tours of the John Muir House start every hour from 1 to 4 P.M. Wednesday through Sunday. Admission is 50 cents for persons over 15 years of age.

CROSSING SAN FRANCISCO BAY

Four bridges span San Francisco Bay to connect Marin County, the city, and the peninsula with the East Bay. Construction of a fifth bridge, the Southern Crossing, is scheduled to begin in 1972. This will extend from San Francisco to Alameda and will be the only cable-stayed bridge in the country. Eight lanes will span 14½ miles, 6 miles over water.

Recent one-way toll collections have helped the flow of traffic on the bridges; tolls are paid by westbound motorists only.

• North of San Francisco is the 2-layered Richmond-San Rafael Bridge. Opened to traffic in 1956, the bridge has 2 cantilevers, 36 trusses, and 36 girder spans. It is 5½ miles long and bears 3 lanes of traffic each way. Toll is 75 cents on this "swaybacked" bridge.

• Completed in 1936, the San Francisco-Oakland Bay Bridge is a combination of cantilevered and suspension sections divided by an island. From San Francisco, two suspension bridges are joined at a central anchorage. The roadway follows a tunnel through Yerba Buena Island, coming out on a 1,400-foot cantilever span followed by a series of truss bridges. The bridge is in two levels (east bound traffic travels on lower deck, westbound traffic on upper deck) and altogether extends 8¼ miles. Toll is 50 cents.

• South of the Bay Bridge is the San Mateo-Hayward Bridge, built in 1967 to replace an older crossing. This bridge extends almost 7 miles over one of the wider parts of the bay and has won several awards for its design. The 4-lane lower trestle expands to a 6-lane steel box girder bridge with a vertical plate deck. This was designed to be the top flange of the girder and to participate in carrying the load rather than adding to it. The toll is 70 cents.

• The Dumbarton Bridge, extending from Menlo Park to Fremont, was opened to traffic in 1927. It extends 6½ miles, but only a little over 1 mile across water. The 2-lane bridge is a vertical lift span. A 70-cent toll is collected on the east side.

DOUBLE-DECKED San Francisco-Oakland Bay Bridge passes through a tunnel, spans 8¼ miles.

THE NORTH BAY COUNTIES

Sausalito • Pt. Reyes Seashore • Russian River
Wine Country • Clear Lake

Fishing Clear Lake

North of San Francisco and the East Bay are the counties of Marin, Sonoma, Napa, and Lake—all of which present a startlingly varied cross-section of California.

Marin County, for instance, houses many San Francisco commuters, while the more northerly parts of this region have remained a peaceful seat of agriculture. The climate ranges from the foggy cool of the rugged coast to the cloudless heat of the flat Napa Valley. Because of the variations in climate, agricultural pursuits include sheep ranches, vineyards, dairy farms, and fruit orchards.

New and sometimes experimental architecture in Marin gives way to century-old stonework in Napa and Sonoma. And the region has a number of resort areas (such as Lake Berryessa and Clear Lake) used for the most part as weekend retreats by Bay Area residents.

The North Bay Counties are crisscrossed by many connecting state highways, most of which are well-surfaced and well-designed. They do not as a general rule carry heavy traffic during the week. U.S. Highway 101, the major thoroughfare, heads north across the Golden Gate Bridge and has a heavy flow of traffic, especially during commute hours in Marin County.

MARIN COUNTY

Many visitors to the San Francisco Bay Area find Marin County the surprise treat of their visit. Sausalito and Tiburon offer unusual shops, good restaurants, and lots of bay and boat watching. At Angel Island you can picnic in a quiet and relatively undeveloped park. If you're interested in the beach, there are Stinson and Pt. Reyes National Seashore; or you can stroll through groves of redwoods at Muir Woods.

Vista Point

Just off the Golden Gate Bridge on the Marin County side, a spacious parking area affords a fine panorama of the bridge, the bay, and the San Francisco skyline.

From Vista Point, you can walk out on the bridge; or follow a pedestrian underpass at either the parking area or the north tower for views of the bay or ocean. In the summer you can watch the fog roll into San Francisco. Sometimes as you stand on the bridge, the bay side is clear while the ocean side is covered by a blanket of fog.

Below the bridge, Fort Baker's red-roofed buildings dot the Marin shore. And almost directly beneath

Inglenook Winery in the Napa Valley

View from Belvedere across Richardson Bay of Marin, Golden Gate Bridge

the north tower, you can see the drab, weathered buildings of Lime Point Lighthouse.

Sausalito

Sausalito's setting has a Mediterranean quality—the harbors are full of small vessels of all sizes and shapes, the hillside architecture is reminiscent of the Italian villa, and the shops and restaurants are concentrated at the water's edge.

Before the building of the Golden Gate Bridge, Sausalito was the transfer point for Marin commuters. They came this far by train, and went on to San Francisco by ferry. (These services stopped in 1937 with the completion of the Golden Gate Bridge; however, ferry service between Tiburon and San Francisco has been recently revived.) The train terminus is now a parking plaza and the handsome old ferry boat *Berkeley*, moored in the slip off Plaza Vina del Mar, a floating retail store.

At the north end of town two other old ferries, the *Vallejo* and the *City of Seattle*, remain afloat. However, both are privately owned and are not open to the public.

Steep Sausalito contains some of the most interest-

ing hillside houses ever built. Narrow tree-lined streets crisscross the hill face of town. Houses are built out into space, often supported by ingenious arrangements of posts, beams, and bracing—and so are their auto parking places. You can get a good view of the Sausalito terrain and the bay from the dining deck of the old Alta Mira Hotel on Bulkley.

Sausalito is a town of small shops. The one conspicuous exception is the old ferry *Berkeley*, now the Trade Fair. Its stock is wide ranging—basketry, lacquerware, pottery, paper goods, small imports. On the rear deck, there are telescopes to focus on San Francisco.

Most complicated (and varied) shopping place is The Village Fair on Bridgeway just north of Plaza Vina del Mar. The interior of this old four-story concrete building is arranged ingeniously in arcades, balconies, staircases, and mezzanines.

On its different levels, there are 40 small specialty shops, some of which contain hand-crafted goods and imports from Europe, Mexico, and India. You can browse through several art galleries or sit down to sip coffee and take in the view.

A walk south from The Village Fair along both sides of Bridgeway reveals one small shop after an-

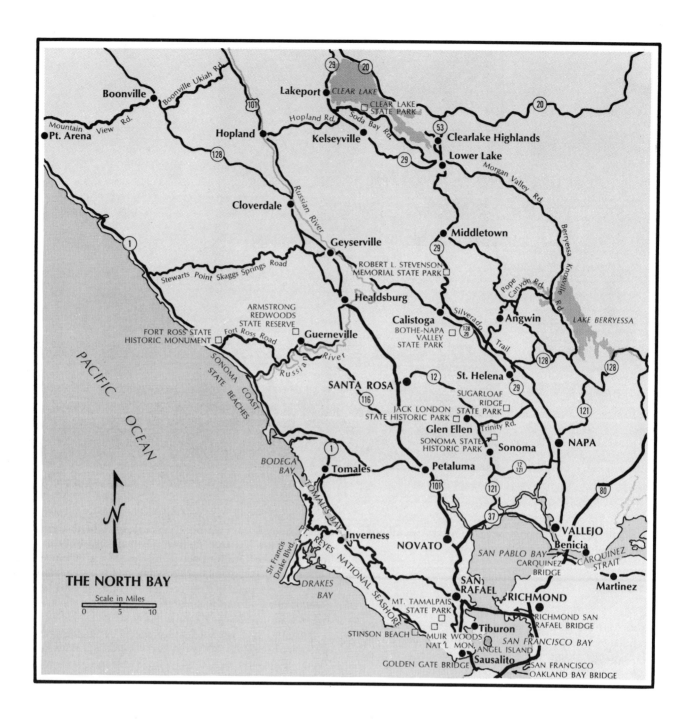

THE NORTH BAY

Scale in Miles

0   5   10

other, each usually in an old building, repainted in cheerful colors. If you're tired, rest under tall Canary Island date palms at the Plaza Vina del Mar.

At the south end of town is a pier supporting several restaurants and a parking lot. From here, you get a marvelous view of Richardson Bay and the San Francisco skyline.

At the north end of town, on Bridgeway, is a curious industrial and maritime wasteland dotted with ship hulls and old shipways, old buildings, and scraps of roadways. During World War II, this was Marinship, an emergency shipyard that launched 93 ships between 1942 and 1945. At the end of Spring Street is the U.S. Army Corps of Engineers San Francisco Bay Model. Used to make precise studies of tides and currents in connection with such changes as extensive land fills, it is open to the public Monday through Friday from 8 A.M. to 4:30 P.M.

Tiburon

A more compact edition of Sausalito, Tiburon sits on the shores of Richardson Bay, directly opposite Sausalito. To reach Tiburon, take U.S. 101 north from

Sausalito to Tiburon Boulevard.

Follow Tiburon Boulevard down to the water and park your car in one of several parking areas. Main Street's first block is Tiburon's downtown—shoulder-to-shoulder shops, art galleries, and some view-of-the-water restaurants. If you want to continue south on Main Street you will pass Corinthian Island (no longer an island) on your way to the foot of Belvedere hill.

Beach Road will take you over Belvedere Lagoon, and past the San Francisco Yacht Club and the old, shingled headquarters of the Belvedere Land Company, in business since 1889.

Angel Island State Park

Part of the fun of going to Angel Island is how you get there. A tour boat at pier 43½ at Fisherman's Wharf or a ferry from Tiburon will take you to the Island in the morning and pick you up in the afternoon. Or you can make the trip in a private boat.

At Ayala Cove, the entrance to Angel Island, there are picnic facilities, beaches for sunning (no swimming is allowed), and a grassy softball field. Bicycle rentals are available (summer only), and there are posted maps of hiking trails. If you take the 5½ mile sightseeing tour of the island, you'll pass through former military areas not open to the public.

Mount Tamalpais

Fine as the views may be from hillcrests in Sausalito and Tiburon, they are even more expansive from the top of Mount Tamalpais.

"Mount Tam" is one of the few places close to downtown San Francisco which has retained a pastoral beauty and which is still open to public use. Part of it is in Muir Woods National Monument, part in Mount Tamalpais State Park, part in water company land (most of which remains open to hikers and fishermen). Only in a few out-of-the-way spots do you encounter fenced private property.

Within the public parts of this land, the roads to the peaks, to Muir Woods, to Stinson Beach, and back to Mill Valley and U.S. 101 are clearly marked. The network of trails about the mountain also is plainly posted.

There are several approaches. You can go north from San Francisco across the bridge and take the underpass (clearly marked) beyond Marin City to State Highway 1. The approach from the west is via State 1, near Stinson Beach, where the Panoramic Highway runs out to the ocean. From the northwest, take the Fairfax-Bolinas Road south from Fairfax.

Mount Tamalpais State Park is open the year around. With the exception of Bootjack Campground, Pantoll Campground, and Alice Eastwood Group Camp, the park closes ½ hour after sundown and opens ½ hour before sunrise.

Muir Woods

Always cool and green, the 502-acre national monument named for the famous naturalist John Muir preserves a stand of virgin coast redwoods (*Sequoia sempervirens*) at the foot of Mount Tamalpais.

For a leisurely walk, follow the ½-mile sign-guided Bootjack Trail. Redwoods and Douglas fir tower above the forest floor, and you will also find tanoak, alder, buckeye, and California laurel, from which one type of bay leaf finds its way into spice jars.

The central part of the park and most of its paths are on a relatively level stretch of forest floor. If you want to do some exploring off the main trail, there are two trails that climb high up the canyon wall to

TRAIL on Angel Island leads to century-old fortress, crosses parade ground of former military camp.

lookout points and a panoramic view to either side of the Golden Gate.

Muir Woods is open daily during daylight hours. Admission is 50 cents for those 16 and over, or you can use your annual federal recreation passport. The monument has no campgrounds or picnic area.

The park is on the Grayline Tour from San Francisco. In summer, it is apt to be quite crowded unless you choose to visit during early morning or late afternoon hours. You can reach Muir Woods via State 1 and the Panoramic Highway. The road into the park, like all those flanking Mount Tamalpais, is narrow and winds tortuously up the long grade from sea level. Its innumerable blind curves require cautious driving.

Stinson Beach

On the ocean shore below Mount Tamalpais, the Stinson Beach sand spit curves offshore for 3 miles beyond the town of Stinson Beach. The town itself is a sidewalkless stretch of small buildings. Its homes spread down the sand spit and up into the hills behind.

At Stinson Beach State Park there is swimming, fishing, picnicking, and beachcombing. You will find the beach crowded on most weekends, but if you drive part way out along the spit and walk even farther, you will have a stretch of beach all to yourself, even on a hot midsummer's day.

The beaches offer a fine sand and a mild surf good for swimming. For the fisherman, perch, bass, eel, cabezon, and smelt are fairly abundant. Trails lead up toward Mount Tamalpais from the water's edge.

State 1 swings north from Stinson Beach around Bolinas Lagoon, where the clamming is good and the waterfowl plentiful. In early morning, you'll see birds wading just a few feet from your car, while kingfishers fly overhead. Most of the birds move on in late winter; however, herons and egrets stay to nest nearby at Audubon Canyon Ranch. The Ranch is open to the public from March 1 to July 5. Visitors are welcome from 10 A.M. to 4 P.M. Saturday and Sunday.

The town of Bolinas rests on its small peninsula, looking like a transplanted stretch of New England coast. It has an admixture of retired mariners and summer dwellers. From it, at low tide, you can walk out on Duxbury Reef, a half submerged needle rock that stretches a mile out to sea from the northern end of Bolinas Beach.

Samuel P. Taylor State Park

At Samuel P. Taylor State Park you can picnic or camp under second-growth redwoods by the side of Lagunitas Creek. There are shallow spots in the creek where youngsters may wade, and a basin is deep enough for swimming. Other facilities include hiking

and riding trails. A corral and watering troughs are available at Devils' Gulch Camp Grounds.

Besides redwoods, you'll see Douglas fir, tanbark oak, and red alder. Wildflowers are plentiful during spring and summer, and park animals include the black-tailed deer, raccoons, and gray foxes. To reach Samuel P. Taylor State Park follow Sir Francis Drake Boulevard from either San Rafael or Tomales Bay into the park.

POINT REYES PENINSULA

Straight up the coast about 30 miles from San Francisco is a triangular peninsula set apart from its surroundings by the San Andreas fault. Authorized in 1962 for 53,000 acres, Point Reyes National Seashore can be easily reached by U.S. Highway 101 and Sir Francis Drake Boulevard or by State 1.

The peninsula has a remarkably colorful history. The Coast Miwok Indians lived here and numerous mounds mark village sites, particularly along the shores of Tomales Bay where the villagers gathered the abundant shellfish.

In 1578, Sir Francis Drake landed his ship, the *Golden Hind*, in a place that sounds very much like Drake's Bay. Drake was met by Coast Miwoks and may have given them the Ming porcelains that have since been found in village mounds. Point Reyes Peninsula has also been the site of 57 shipwrecks.

The peninsula is unlike the adjacent coast in several ways. Most important, perhaps, is the weather—some areas receive up to 55 inches of rain a year. The long hook of the point catches rainstorms that supply the springs, creeks, and lakes with an abundance of water. And the winds that make the Point Reyes Lighthouse (not open to the public) one of the windiest points along the coast also sweep across the low, unprotected seaward meadows, keeping them cool in summer and frost-free in winter.

Among the rich vegetation are several species of plants unique to the peninsula. The protected hills and valleys of Inverness Ridge are the most southerly habitat of the mountain beaver, and untouched stands of Douglas fir with six foot diameters are not unusual.

Since the park is divided by private lands, there are two distinct areas open to the visitor. (About one-half of the 53,000 acres allotted to the park is now publicly owned.) You reach the major beaches and the dairylands through Inverness to the north, the Bear Valley trails and the hilly forest of Inverness Ridge through park headquarters near Olema off State 1.

The area around Inverness, the peninsula's principal community, is not part of the national seashore. The town consists mainly of a couple of general stores and some picturesque frame houses which are weekend summer retreats. Inverness is a good take-off

WAVES THUNDER onto McClure's Beach at the northern end of Pt. Reyes National Seashore. A steep, narrow access trail from parking area leads to this usually deserted cliff-backed beach.

point for boating excursions on Tomales Bay. Boats can be rented at the north end of town or across the bay at Marshall.

The Point Reyes Peninsula is an ideal place for an August, September, or October outing. It reaches another peak of attractiveness in May when many wildflowers are in bloom. In midsummer, chances are you will find yourself shrouded in fog (a condition which prevails all along this coast).

Limited accommodations restrict the peninsula as a vacation area. There are a few campgrounds at Bear Valley, or you can camp at Samuel Taylor State Park, about 6 miles southeast of Point Reyes Station, or at a private campground near Olema.

Bear Valley Trails

Bear Valley Ranch is the biggest single piece of land on the peninsula now in public ownership. On its 7,715 acres more than 40 miles of trails are open to hikers, horsemen, and bicycle riders. There are also a few campsites but camping is by permit only.

From park headquarters the main trail leads 4½ nearly level miles along creeks and through fir groves and meadows to the sea, where picnickers and sun-

bathers are welcome to use the beaches. Where the creek cuts its way through the cliffs, you'll come across tunnels and pocket beaches to explore.

For energetic hikers, there are side trails (some of which are very steep) that lead up from various points along the main trail. The trail up 1,407-foot Mount Wittenberg seems very difficult as you look up from the bottom, but both the walk and the view from the summit are thoroughly enjoyable. On a clear day you can see the entire sweep of Drake's Bay out to distant Point Reyes.

Point Reyes Beach

If you follow Sir Francis Drake Highway as it loops to the southwest beyond Inverness, you'll come to Point Reyes Beach. At both north and south ends of the beach you'll find picnic grounds in the rough grass of the dunes. Water and rest rooms are available. This beach, with its bluffs, its long, unbroken sweep of sand, and its crashing waves, is the most impressive one on the peninsula. The surf is always too rough for swimming, but you can walk, or just sit and admire the scene.

CLAMMERS shovel through wet mud while tide is out to dislodge stubborn gapers at mouth of Tomales Bay.

Drake's Beach

If you take a left turn near the south entrance to Point Reyes Beach, you soon reach Drake's Beach—tamer but equally beautiful. Near the parking lot is a stone marker that states this is the spot where Sir Francis Drake is believed to have beached the *Golden Hind.* Looking down the long horseshoe of the bay you see the rolling white cliffs which may be those described by Drake's chaplain.

McClure's Beach

This beach, at the northern end of the peninsula, is usually almost deserted, as the access trail is steep and narrow. There is no swimming here, but there are plenty of driftwood logs for fires and rocks for shelter from the wind.

Tomales Bay State Park

Tomales Bay State Park, just north of Inverness, is not part of the national seashore, but it includes some fine stretches of land. The flat, usually surfless beaches open onto the protected bay, where sailboats move back and forth in front of the smooth mainland hills. The water gets deeper slowly and is excellent for small children to wade in.

THE SONOMA COAST

The Sonoma Coast is a shorter and less developed counterpart to its more famous neighbor to the north, the Mendocino Coast (see page 54). Its principal attractions are a series of beach parks, awesome scenery, and Fort Ross, the last surviving sign of 19th-century Russian incursions into California.

Sonoma Coast State Beach

Sonoma Coast State Beach runs north from Bodega Bay to the mouth of the Russian River along State 1 and takes in almost 60,000 feet of ocean frontage. Beachcombers and fishermen in particular will find this stretch of coastline fascinating. There is no ocean swimming here because of the strong undertow.

Camping and picnicking are permitted at Wright's Beach and just picnicking at Rock Point Roadside Rest. Goat Rock, at the northern end of the park, is a popular daytime beach with fine sand, and fresh and saltwater fishing.

Fort Ross

Thirteen miles north of the junction of State Highways 1 and 116 at Jenner, the stout wooden buildings of Fort Ross sit high on a headland. Both a state park and national monument, Fort Ross originally was the American outpost for the Russian fur traders of the 19th century.

Originally the park contained four buildings within its towering stockade walls, each of them reconstructed in this century. Still standing and open to the public are two blockhouses. The old commandant's log house suffered a roof fire in the summer of 1971 and is temporarily closed until repairs can be made. It serves as a museum, having on display artifacts and documents related to the area's successive occupation by the native Kashia Pomo Indians, the Russians, and finally the Americans.

Across the highway, which cuts through the park, stood the Russian Orthodox chapel. Until it was destroyed by fire in October of 1970, it was the oldest Russian Orthodox chapel still standing in the United States. The chapel, originally constructed in 1825, will eventually be reconstructed.

Below the headland, along Fort Ross Creek, the state maintains picnic facilities. A small use fee is charged. Park hours are 8 A.M. to 5 P.M. Saturday, Sunday, and holidays; 10 A.M. to 5 P.M. weekdays. Summer hours are 8 A.M. to 6 P.M. daily.

RUSSIAN RIVER

To the summer visitors who have swarmed there since the early days of San Francisco, "The River" is the

12-mile cluster of resorts from Mirabel Park to Monte Rio. Less known is the surrounding country—defined on the map by a sprawling "H," with the Russian River as its crossbar and U.S. 101 (through the Santa Rosa Valley) and State 1 (along the coast) as its vertical members.

The most direct approach to the river from the south is U.S. 101 to Cotati (48 miles from San Francisco), then left on State 116 to Sebastopol and to the river.

For a more leisurely approach, take either the Guerneville Road from Santa Rosa, the Fulton-Trenton Road (3½ miles north of Santa Rosa), the Eastside Road (3½ miles south of Healdsburg), or the Westside Road from Healdsburg to Hacienda. Other minor roads that crisscross the whole area make pleasant country driving.

West and north on the river's great semicircle, the mountains rise and seem nearly inaccessible. You may explore them on a drive up narrow Mill Creek Road that starts 1½ miles from Healdsburg on Westside Road. Its 4 miles of pavement take you up into the tangy air and the stillness of dense second-growth redwood and Douglas fir, logged-over slopes, and virgin forest in Mill Creek Canyon. Beyond the pavement's end, you may hike up this road in dry weather, scaling the steep ridge high above the canyon.

Along the river

All roads to the Russian River eventually lead to Guerneville. It is the center of the river resort area which extends east as far as Mirabel Park and west to Jenner, at the river's mouth.

You will find restaurants and places to stay overnight in this section. During the summer season, this is the scene of bustling activity, with thousands of vacationers participating in a variety of resort activity. (Make reservations well ahead of time if you plan to stay overnight.)

Farther upstream there is good canoeing where the Russian River flows through the Alexander Valley. With a durable canoe or kayak you can have some pleasant canoeing between Asti and Healdsburg (where canoes can be rented) and Guerneville. River trips can last from four hours to two days. The sun can be very hot on the river in the summer, so take some protective clothing. Be sure to include drinking water and a picnic lunch.

The river is fairly quiet during the rest of the year. Roads are uncrowded, and there are few visitors.

The steelhead and salmon fishermen begin to arrive in late fall. During the steelhead fishing season (November through February), resort owners and sporting goods stores keep track of the steelhead runs from the time the fish are reported crossing the river bar until they pass Healdsburg upstream.

In late May and early June American shad begin their spring migrations on the Russian River. The most successful shad fishing is in the same pools and riffles that produce steelhead in winter. Maps showing the location of the best pools are usually available in local tackle shops. Bait shops or river resorts can tell you where the fishing is currently most promising.

Armstrong Redwoods State Reserve

Armstrong Redwoods State Reserve is 2 miles north of Guerneville. You may drive a short loop through dimly-lit aisles among ferns and the giant trees, or walk the trails—the only ones in the whole area that were laid out expressly for hiking—that extend to the park's limits.

Another hiking possibility is the road that leads to the Mount Jackson fire lookout. Called the Sweetwater Springs Road, it starts near the entrance to Armstrong Woods. It is paved for a mile, as far as a quicksilver mine. Beyond is a narrow, climbing dirt road—slow driving, better for hiking—that continues for 2 miles through fairly open chaparral to a fire lookout on top. From the top on clear days, you can survey the mountains, the river canyon, and the Santa Rosa Valley. You may startle a deer or a cottontail—the hills are full of wildlife.

NARROW and tree-lined Russian River offers good canoeing with occasional rapids, brush obstructions.

STEADY AFTERNOON breezes provide fine sailing on Howarth Memorial Park's 32-acre lake. Santa Rosa's most popular park also has picnic areas, trails, tennis courts, children's playground.

IN AND AROUND SANTA ROSA

Howarth Memorial Park is Santa Rosa's biggest and most attractive park. A 152-acre tree-shaded retreat, it sits at the foot of the Coast Range.

If you are headed north or south on U.S. 101, the park is a fine rest and picnic spot. An imaginative and attractive 20-acre children's area includes a pony ride, an animal farm, a merry-go-round, a miniature train, and playground areas. All rides cost 15 cents; the other attractions are free.

A feature of the main park is a beautiful 32-acre lake. Motorboats are prohibited, but you can rent sailboats, canoes, and rowboats for $1 per hour. The park also has picnic areas, several miles of hiking trails, tennis courts, and a softball field.

The park entrance is on Summerfield Road between Sonoma Avenue and Montgomery Drive, about 5 minutes from the freeway. Howarth Park is open daily the year around; however, the amusement rides and boat rental office are open daily in the summer and on weekends only during spring and fall.

North of Santa Rosa, just east of U.S. 101 at Windsor, is a horse barn restored to its original Victorian elegance. Mount Weske Stable, constructed in the early 1890's for Adolph Weske's trotters, required 16 carloads of redwood lumber, rolls of steel rods, and 52 kegs of square nails. The octagonal barn is 105 feet tall and is the same distance wide.

Today the barn is a stable where 50 horses can be boarded. Horse shows are held occasionally and on weekends groups take riding lessons.

To reach Mount Weske Stable, take the Windsor exit from U.S. 101 to Brooks Road; a sign on the road marks the Stable at 10500 Brooks Road. Visitors are welcome from 10 A.M. to 6 P.M. daily except Monday.

SONOMA VALLEY

Historically, Sonoma is one of the most interesting towns in California. It is the site of Mission San Francisco Solano de Sonoma, last and northernmost of the 21 missions founded by the Franciscan fellows of Fray Junipero Serra. It was the headquarters for General Mariano Vallejo, the Mexican administrator at the time of the Bear Flag Revolt. It is where the Hungarian Agoston Haraszthy laid the groundwork for some premium California wines at his Buena Vista winery (see page 52), and Sonoma was the last home of author Jack London.

Sonoma

The town of Sonoma centers around a spacious central plaza. Across from the northeast corner of the plaza is Mission San Francisco Solano, founded on July 4, 1823. In 1911-12 the state restored the crumbling structure and made it a state historical monument and museum. Here you can see historic church vestments, early photographs and documents, and 62 oil paintings of the missions. The mission chapel is preserved, although it is no longer used for religious services. Museum hours are 9 A.M. to 5 P.M. daily.

Across Spain Street, the Blue Wing Inn survives as one of the early buildings in the pueblo. West on Spain Street from the mission, you pass the Bear Flag National Historical Monument (in the northeast corner of the plaza park), the Sonoma Barracks, the servants' wing of Casa Grande (Vallejo's first home, most of which was destroyed by fire in 1867), the Swiss Hotel (still in use as a restaurant), and the home of Salvador Vallejo, Mariano's brother.

Two blocks west, then north on Third Street West is the home of General Mariano Vallejo. The name of Vallejo's Sonoma home, Lachryma Montis ("tear of the mountain"), was suggested by the natural spring in the area. Adobe brick walls were covered with wood, so what looks like a wooden cottage is surprisingly cool inside on a hot day. A section of wall near the porch entrance has been cut away and faced with glass to give visitors a better idea of the construction. Also on the site is a handsome old warehouse, built in 1852 of timber and bricks shipped around Cape Horn. The Vallejo Home Historical Monument is open daily from 10 A.M. to 5 P.M.

Jack London State Historic Park

The Jack London State Historic Park is situated in the hills above the tiny community of Glen Ellen. You can visit the huge stone house built by London's wife, Charmian, which is now a museum of the author's personal and professional life.

The ruins of the Wolf House, which London planned but never occupied, are also in the park at the end of a ¾-mile trail which begins at the museum. London's grave is near the ruins.

To get to London State Historic Park from Sonoma, take State 12 north from town, turn west at Agua Caliente Road, then north again on Arnold Drive to Glen Ellen. A sign in Glen Ellen points to London Ranch Road. The park is open daily from 10 A.M to 5 P.M.

Sugarloaf Ridge State Park

A 1,500-acre preserve of forest, field, and stream that reaches up oak-covered hills has been set aside as Sugarloaf Ridge State Park. The park has campsites and picnic facilities, hiking and riding trails, meadows, and sites of old farm buildings.

You enter the park by Adobe Canyon Road, a county road off State 12. The park gate is 2½ miles farther, with a camping area (picnicking facilities available) a mile past the gate on a steep oiled road.

SUGARLOAF RIDGE State Park, in Sonoma Valley, offers delightful picnicking among bay and live oak trees.

Numerous springs support a resident trout population, but the fish are wily and hard to hook.

THE WINE COUNTRY

Napa and Sonoma counties are the backbone of the North Coast wine districts. Between them, they contain most (not all, by any means) of the premium California wineries. Their origins go back to the pueblo days of California, and they have antecedents in the earliest mission vineyards which proved the capacity of the state as a wine-growing region.

The best time to visit the wine country is late September and early October. This is the most active period, when the crush takes place—the initial fermenting of the new year's wines. The heady aroma of newly crushed grapes burdens the warm afternoon air. Vines, stripped of their clusters of grapes, are tinged with gold and scarlet. Inside the wineries, in spite of hurried labor over the about-to-ferment grapes, amiable guides welcome visitors as nonchalantly as they might in the still days of winter when the wines take care of themselves.

The greatest concentration of wineries open to visitors is along State Highway 29 north and south of the unhurried town of St. Helena. However, if you want to start with the beginnings, visit the Buena Vista winery in Sonoma.

Buena Vista's vineyards were founded in 1832 by Agoston Haraszthy, who earned his title of "Father of California Viticulture" with the selection and importing of thousands of cuttings from the finest vineyards in France, Germany, Italy, and his native Hungary. Across a small creek from the original fine old stone buildings of the winery, shaded picnic tables are provided for the use of visitors. To get to the winery, take East Napa Street east to Old Winery Road; turn north and follow the road to its end.

St. Helena is the center of Napa Valley wine making. On its southern outskirts you can make an interesting comparison between the tiny Heitz Cellars and the larger Louis Martini Winery. They are side-by-side on the east side of the highway. Sutter Home winery is opposite them.

On the northern outskirts of St. Helena, Beringer Brothers, Christian Brothers, and Charles Krug are clustered close together, each in a fascinating building. Beringer Brothers also has an elaborate series of tunnels hewn out of the hillside by Chinese coolies. Farther north, near Calistoga on Larkmead Lane, Hanns Kornell Champagne Cellars is a tradition-oriented and colorful place.

Two other fine wineries are in Rutherford several miles south of St. Helena. Beaulieu is just east of the highway, while Inglenook is set almost a mile west of the road.

A small winery named Mayacamas, after the mountains that separate the Napa and Sonoma valleys, is tucked away in the hills high above the Napa Valley floor. Getting to the winery requires some perseverance, but in addition to offering a tour of the premises, it provides you with an opportunity to see some fine panoramic views down into the valley, and (if you climb to its highest vineyard) south to San Francisco. Mount Veeder Road will take you to the winery.

For a complete listing of wineries which welcome visitors, and for hours, write the Wine Institute, 717 Market Street, San Francisco, for the free booklet, *Wine Wonderland*. Sunset's *California Wine Country* gives a brief description of all California wineries plus location maps and visitors' hours.

Byways for driving

The fame of Napa and Sonoma counties rests, deservedly, upon their noble wines. To the delight of people who do much of their driving on freeways, Napa and Sonoma also provide hundreds of miles of rural roads. The scenery in the valleys and on the mountains which frame them is not awesome. Rather, it is the quiet beauty of a lush agricultural region. Narrow and unhurried, the roads wind past vineyards and orchards, detour around farmhouses, and slip unobtrusively across hills wooded with oak and eucalyptus, or with conifers.

For a half-day 60-mile loop trip around St. Helena head north on State 29, toward Calistoga. About four miles beyond St. Helena, on the left, is the Old Bale Mill built in 1846 for the convenience of all nearby residents who needed their grain ground into meal. You can explore the rooms inside and view the grinding stones that were active for more than 35 years. A small area alongside the huge, overshot wheel is a county park open to picnickers.

Another mile north is the entrance to the Bothe-Napa Valley State Park. It has more than a thousand wooded acres of broad-leafed trees and conifers, and second-growth redwoods which extend west into the hills. Its facilities include camping and picnicking sites, hiking trails, and a swimming pool. Ritchie Creek, which runs through the park, provides fishing.

Calistoga, just east of State 29, has a scattering of hot springs, mineral springs, and steaming geysers. As you head north from Calistoga on State 29, you'll soon get up into a wooded region with a surprising number of pines mixed in with oaks, madrones, and toyons. Very near the summit a small state park commemorates the place where Robert Louis Stevenson spent a two-month honeymoon in 1880, and also gathered material put down in his book, *Silverado Squatters*. A fire trail, in about a half-mile, leads to some remnants of his cabin and the old Silverado Mine. It continues uphill for another 3½ miles to the lookout on top of this 4,344-foot peak that Stevenson called the "Mont Blanc of the Coast Range."

Just beyond the park State 29 coasts down through gradually broadening valleys to Middletown, a small trading center which is also a gateway to the so-called "mountain" resorts of Lake County. You can leave the beaten track at Middletown and head southeast on Butts Canyon Road (a lonelier road than the highway) leading to Aetna Springs, Pope Valley, and Lake Berryessa.

Mount Veeder Road is a challenging choice. It is tightly winding and not especially smooth, but ridgetop views compensate for its bumpy stretches. About a mile north of Napa, turn off State 29 to the west at Redwood Road. Follow Redwood Road to the junction with Mount Veeder Road.

Spring Mountain Road offers a somewhat less trying ride without any great sacrifice in the scenery. To take this detour off State 29-128, turn west at St. Helena onto Madrona Avenue (a few blocks north of the business district). Drive two blocks, then turn north where a sign indicates Santa Rosa is 20 miles away. You are on Spring Mountain Road—dirt surfaced, narrow, winding, and climbing.

CLEAR LAKE

Local residents will tell you that Clear Lake is the largest lake entirely within California (Tahoe is bigger, but not wholly within the state). It is a natural

RHINE HOUSE at Beringers serves as visitor center, tasting room.

CLEAR LAKE'S placid waters invite swimmers, boaters, fishermen. For dramatic views of lake, drive the higher roads around the southern tip.

lake, fairly shallow, about 19 miles long and up to 7½ miles wide, surrounded by many well-kept resorts and a great variety of recreation.

The summer throngs begin arriving in May, and from then through September the resorts and roads near the lake are crowded. If you visit Clear Lake during the summer season, be sure to make reservations ahead of time. (A free listing of places to stay is available by writing the Lake County Chamber of Commerce, Lakeport, California.)

The direct route from the Bay Area to the southern tip of the lake (about 120 miles from San Francisco) is via State 29 through the Napa Valley. Clear Lake can also be approached from the west through Hopland.

Anglers flock to Clear Lake for some good bass fishing in spring and early summer. However, October with its balmy fall weather and scarcity of swimmers, speedboats, and water skiers can offer the best fishing of the year.

Lakeport, on the west shore, is one of the lake's boating centers, and there is a large public launching ramp, a water ski ramp, a public pier, and a park with picnicking and swimming facilities. If you're interested in Lake County's history and the lore of the Pomo Indians, look into the museum on Third Street, near the old vine-covered County Courthouse (a landmark).

Clear Lake State Park (camping, picnicking), is just south. Most of the park is on a high, forested promontory overlooking Soda Bay and Mount Konocti to the south.

The lake's largest resort concentration is a few miles north of Lower Lake. From this center around Clearlake Highlands and Clearlake Park, you can continue north around the lake on paved State Highway 53. This "inland" route takes you through sparse oak forest and grazing land and returns to the shore and State Highway 20. State 20 follows the shore north and around the "top" of the lake; main resort centers are at Clearlake Oaks, Lucerne, and Nice.

LAKE BERRYESSA

Lake Berryessa is 80 miles from San Francisco by way of Interstate 80. Turn north on Interstate 505 just beyond Vacaville to the Winters cut-off; then follow State Highway 128 west to Monticello Dam at the south end of the lake. For a more scenic route, take State Highway 121 through Napa County.

Lake Berryessa's shoreline is federal land administered by Napa County under a 50-year lease from the Bureau of Reclamation. The county, in turn, has granted 20 to 50-year sub-leases on portions of this land to seven private resorts, under the supervision of the Lake Berryessa Park Commission. Bank fishing and picnicking are permitted along the shoreline except on the east side which has been closed to the public because of fire hazard.

NORTH ALONG THE COAST

**Fishing Harbors • Mendocino • The Beaches
Pastoral Valleys • Redwood National Park**

Mendocino Coast

The California coastline north from San Francisco is dramatic—with steep rocky headlands shrouded by fog in the summer and battered by howling storms in the winter. North of Eureka, the coastal redwoods crowd the shore and stand tall against the clouds, rain, and fog.

The narrow coastal shelf is rugged, haunting country which was well suited to the New Englanders who settled here to log and to fish. It is still well suited to the man who wants some tumult from his environment. More than a century after the first mill equipment and men arrived at the mouth of the Big River, logging and commercial fishing still go on. Also there are sheep ranches, and inland there are apple orchards and vineyards.

If you are a camper, beachcomber, fisherman, auto explorer, artist, or photographer, you will find pleasure along the northern coast.

THE MENDOCINO COAST

Coastal Mendocino drowses contentedly in the warm backwash of the 19th century. Its towns have stayed small and spaced well apart. In fact, the coastal region is less populous now than it was at the height of the fishing and logging era of the 1920's and 1930's.

The commercial center and only coast city of any size between San Francisco and Eureka is Fort Bragg

(about 5,000 population). Along with neighboring Noyo, it is the heart of the regional lumbering and fishing industries. Of the smaller communities along the shore, Mendocino is the most noted and the most crowded during the summer.

Between the towns, sheep ranches and farms keep the thread of population going. As in the towns, the houses and other buildings are in the main Victorian, built by Victorian New Englanders. Infrequently, a very new building emphasizes the age and stability of the area.

Remnants of the past are visible along the jumbled shore. Rusting stacks of abandoned lumber mills cling to desolate river banks. At the tops of bluffs, a few weathered timbers mark the site of a chute from which lumber was loaded onto steam schooners. In overgrown fields, rough vacant buildings left by loggers await collapse.

Weather

Your best chances of finding good outing weather are in May and early June when the azaleas and rhododendrons are in bloom and summer traffic is not, or during September and October when the weather is balmy and the roads and campgrounds not so crowded. The tourist season runs from Memorial Day to Labor Day, even though the coastal fog bank

Prairie Creek State Park

Village of Ferndale in lower Eel River Valley

spends a greater part of its time ashore during the summer months.

The rainy season begins around mid-October, with most of the annual rainfall of 35 inches occurring from December to May. Most winter days are in the 40-50° range; summer temperatures often get into the 70's.

Highways and roads

For one hundred crooked miles, State Highway 1 clings to the seaward edge of Mendocino County. Much of it is two lanes, within a mile of the sea and almost always in sight of it. The highway dips and twists across sharply ridged country and around deep coves. High and low bridges take you across the mouths of Mendocino's many rivers and creeks.

Most of the land you pass through is fenced. There are few side roads to explore and only in a few places can you get down to the shore. But the fences are an appealing awkward and various lot and the views beyond them remarkably varied because of the coast's rugged nature. The public beaches, scattered along the road's length from Gualala to Fort Bragg, take in the whole range from flat, sandy coves to rugged, tunneled headlands.

The 20 miles from Albion to Fort Bragg are the most heavily populated and the most heavily traveled of the 100 miles in Mendocino County.

To reach the Mendocino Coast, you can join State 1 at its Leggett junction with U.S. Highway 101 north of Fort Bragg, or come up the Sonoma coast.

Two other routes provide easy access to the coast. State Highway 128 meanders north and west from Cloverdale on U.S. 101 in Sonoma County, passing through miles of rolling orchard and vineyard country before it winds into redwood forests to become a peaceful path through the towering trees. You pass through several small hamlets along the 57 miles of well-paved, two-lane highway.

The other route, State Highway 20, is more direct and less inhabited. It leaves U.S. 101 at Willits and joins State 1 just south of Fort Bragg-Noyo. There are no incorporated towns along its 35 miles. Jackson State Forest preserves a fine stand of redwood and Douglas fir along the roadway. On any of these roads, you will encounter a good number of logging trucks.

Accommodations

There is no over-abundance of accommodations on the coast; however, you have your choice of old-time establishments or modern motels.

Two inns in Little River and the hotel in Mendocino recall the nostalgia of the past. If you wish to stay at one of these places, reservations are a must. Reservations are also advisable, especially during the

THE NORTH COAST

Scale in Miles
0   5   10   15

Smith River

Crescent City

JEDEDIAH SMITH
REDWOODS STATE PARK

REDWOOD

DEL NORTE COAST
REDWOODS STATE PARK

NATIONAL

PARK

Orick

PRAIRIE CREEK
REDWOODS
STATE PARK

PATRICKS POINT
STATE PARK

TRINIDAD STATE BEACH

LITTLE RIVER
STATE BEACH

HUMBOLDT

EUREKA

BAY

Fernbridge

Ferndale

Fortuna

Eel River

Mattole Road

HUMBOLDT
REDWOODS
STATE PARK

PACIFIC

Garberville

RICHARDSON GROVE
STATE PARK

OCEAN

Leggett

MACKERRICHER
STATE PARK

Fort Bragg

Willits

RUSSIAN GULCH
STATE PARK

Mendocino

VAN DAMME STATE PARK

Comptche

Flynn
Creek
Road

Orr Springs Road

Ukiah

Albion

PAUL M. DIMMICK
STATE RECREATION AREA

HENDY WOODS STATE PARK

Boonville

Manchester

MANCHESTER STATE BEACH

Pt. Arena

Mountain
View Road

summer and on weekends, at any of the comfortable motels in Fort Bragg, Mendocino, and Little River. For a listing of places to stay, write to the Fort Bragg-Mendocino Chamber of Commerce, P.O. Box 1141, Fort Bragg, California 95437.

Parks and campgrounds

Getting down to the shore or back into the forest is mainly a matter of getting to a state or local park, most of which have fine camping or picnicking facilities along with abundant scenery.

In the town of Mendocino, Heeser Drive offers a fine place to picnic or watch the ocean at its endless task of destroying its own shore. The drive is on a rocky point west of town where the bluffs are comprised of elaborately carved and tunneled rock suited to exploration on foot (not for children). In a few places you can get down onto pebble beaches to launch a skin-diving foray or merely to hunt for flotsam.

Van Damme State Park is located on Little River (a small stream along which campsites, a scenic drive, and hiking trails are located). One of the trails leads to an ancient pygmy forest of stunted conifers in the southeast quarter of the park. A recreation hall, playing field, and pebble beach round out the activities of the coastal park. Skin-diving for abalone and rockfish is a popular activity in the 52° waters of the cove.

Russian Gulch State Park lies along the coast just north of the town of Mendocino and extends out onto a wave-scarred headland pocketed with coves, pools, points, and a partially collapsed blow-hole. It offers, in addition to this dramatic edge, an easy hike up Russian Gulch Creek to a lace-like waterfall. The falls are set in second-growth redwoods, Douglas fir, laurel, oak, and hemlock underlain with fields of ferns. The park's 35 campsites are located in the mouth of the canyon, protected from the chilly winds of afternoon and evening. Near the campsites, the beach is broad and the creek shallow, an ideal place for children to splash and wade. Ocean swimming is dangerous, although skin-diving for abalone is a popular sport.

Four miles north of Fort Bragg, MacKerricher Beach State Park offers the same variety of black sand and rocky headland as the other parks. MacKerricher is the best of these beaches for surf fishing (rosetail, perch, rockfish, smelt), but a steep drop-off and rough water make it unsuited for swimming. Four miles of beach and headlands offer an abundance of sea life at low tide. Campsites here are sheltered from the winds by a dense grove of gnarled Bishop pine, shore pine, and tanoak. You can do some fresh-water fishing for trout at Lake Cleone, within the park.

Other places to get down to the water are in Manchester, Anchor Bay, Point Arena, Pudding Creek, and 10 Mile Beach north of Fort Bragg.

If you happen to be in this area on one of those foggy weekends, you can escape the fog by driving 9 miles inland on State 128 to Paul M. Dimmick Wayside Campground. It is in a maturing stand of second-growth redwoods along the banks of the Navarro River. In season, the river produces good catches of steelhead and migrating salmon. This park is open from spring until fall as a campground.

Jackson State Forest on State 20 has more primitive campsites than the parks. For trail information, contact the California Division of Forestry Office in Fort Bragg.

For a complete list of campgrounds along the Mendocino Coast, write to the Fort Bragg-Mendocino Chamber of Commerce or consult Sunset's *Western Campsite Directory*.

Boonville to the coast

About 30 miles inland from the windy Mendocino coast lie the quiet ranches and hillside pastures of the Anderson Valley. The main road through the valley is State 128.

Boonville is the largest town between Cloverdale and the ocean. It was settled in the 1850's, and the people of the town and the surrounding ranches still make their living from the apples they grow and the sheep, cattle, and hogs they raise.

In the spring, apple blossoms and native western azaleas color the valley pink and white against the sheep-cropped green hills. This is the time of the rodeo called "Buck-a-roo Days." Activities include fishing for trout in the Navarro River and its tributaries and camping in the area parks. Another annual event occurs in July when sheep raisers gather to exchange gossip, compete for prizes, and feast on barbecued lamb. This event, held under the tall shade trees of the Mendocino County Fairgrounds, welcomes visitors.

In the fall and winter, steelhead run in the Navarro, and roadside stands sell the fine apples of the valley. A September event is the County Fair and Apple Show—reminiscent of old-time fairs—which draws visitors from all over the West.

Two state parks lie just north of Boonville on State 128. At Indian Creek State Reserve, a 15-acre stand of mature redwoods, you can picnic and fish. No camping is permitted. Hendy Woods State Park is a well-developed forest area that covers 607 acres. Within the park's thick woods are two groves of virgin redwoods saved from the loggers by Joshua P. Hendy, who owned the land. Some of these trees are 300 feet tall. In the summer you can swim and fish in the Navarro River and picnic and camp.

You can reach the coast via State 128, or if you are prepared for a more rugged ride, take Mountain View Road from Boonville. Just south of the junction of Mountain View Road and State 1 is the Point Arena Lighthouse. This is the most powerful lighthouse on the coast and is open to visitors from 1 to 4 P.M. Saturday, Sunday, and holidays.

INTRODUCTION TO BOONT

Like the Hawaiians with their Pidgin and the Cockneys with their rhyming slang, some of the people of Boonville speak a dialect quite their own. It's called Boontling, and when a real Boonter speaks it, there's an uneven lilt and a touch of humor that runs all through the more than 1,000 words of vocabulary that make it up.

Boontling grew up in Boonville in the late 1880's or early 90's when the men would meet in town and try to *shark* (stump) each other with a new Boont word. The origins of some of the words have been lost, since Boontling developed as a spoken language and has only recently been written. A few logical patterns are apparent in word formation.

All through Boontling, names have come to be descriptive nouns. A *Charlie Walker* is a photograph, after the one-legged photographer from Mendocino who took family portraits for the people of Boonville. A big mustache is called a *Tom Bacon* for the man who could reputedly wrap his handlebar mustache around his ears. Horace Greeley's name is used for any journalist, but especially to mean a newspaperman.

The forming of many Boont words took place through a shortening of already existing words and phrases. The word *Boontling* itself is from Boonville lingo. A *relf* is a rail fence, a *hairk* is a hair cut, a *haireem* is a "hairy mouth" or dog, and *skipe* is a clergyman, from sky pilot. Also, by adding the word region to these, a *hairk region* becomes a barbershop, and a *skipe region* is a church.

The remainder of Boontling is made up mostly of words or phrases whose connotation is immediately clear to a Boonter. *Featherlegged* means a know-it-all and comes from the strutting barnyard cocks. *Trashmover,* "big storms," tells something of the winter problems of a rural community.

MENDOCINO'S main street faces ocean, has craft shops, art galleries, and New England architecture.

LUMBERJACK leads parade down Fort Bragg's Main Street during annual Paul Bunyan Days over Labor Day.

From Mendocino to Fort Bragg

The town of Mendocino most clearly retains the flavor of its ancestral New England. Much of the architecture in town is pure Victorian. Be sure to note the Old Masonic Hall at Lansing and Ukiah streets, with its massive redwood sculpture of Father Time and the Maiden.

The residents of the town of Mendocino include a highly competent community of artists. Their work is on display at the Mendocino Art Center (several blocks north of Main Street on Little Lake Street) where several maintain studios or in any of the several art galleries in town. You will see oils, wood blocks, and water colors depicting local architecture and the sea in a variety of styles.

Just north of Mendocino, off State 1 on Ocean Drive, the Fort Bragg Trout Farm maintains a hatchery where rainbow trout are raised. At the fishing pond, you can fish for large trout. Poles and bait are provided and no fishing license is required. Charge for fishing is 25 cents. Picnic facilities are provided. The Trout Farm is open daily from noon to dusk.

North of the Trout Farm on State 1 is the Mendocino Coast Botanical Gardens. Here acres of rhododendrons, fuchsias, azaleas, bulbs, and many other flowering plants and shrubs blend with the rugged coast and the redwood wilderness. The gardens are open daily from 8:30 A.M. to 6 P.M. Entrance fee is $1.00 for adults, 50 cents for children 6 to 12 years of age.

Five miles north of Mendocino is the second most powerful light station on the coast. You can visit Point Cabrillo Lighthouse from 1 to 5 P.M. on Saturday, Sunday, and holidays.

Deep-water fishermen will find charter boats at Noyo and Albion. Both harbors are in deep coves below high bridges. Standard rate is $12.50 per person for a half day of off-shore fishing for salmon. The morning trips start at 7 A.M. and return around noon. Afternoon trips start at 1 P.M. and return at about 5 P.M. The season runs from June until the first week of October (weekend trips only after school resumes). There are few of these boats, each with an average capacity of 8 fishermen, so it is wise to reserve a place in advance.

Noyo maintains a free public launching ramp for boatowners. You can launch for a fee at a commercial ramp in Albion.

In Fort Bragg you can visit the world's second largest operating redwood sawmill. The Boise Cascade Union Lumber Company Region welcomes visitors daily—tours are at 8:30 and 9:30 A.M., noon, 2 and 4 P.M. from June to Labor Day; 2 P.M. only in the off-season. The company maintains an extensive museum of photographs and machinery of California lumbering at the plant site a block west of State 1 on Redwood Avenue.

Over Labor Day weekend the annual Paul Bunyan Days recall the early lumbering era. This three-day celebration includes such special activities as a parade, axe throwing contest, and log-rolling contest.

Touring Redwood Country by rail

You can get a better view of the countryside if you take one of the two passenger-carrying trains which tour the Redwood Country.

The California Western Railroad "Skunk" train links Fort Bragg with Willits. It winds through dark forests of second-growth redwood and Douglas fir, rambles through two tunnels, and rattles across 33 bridges and trestles during the 40-mile trip which is interrupted frequently to pick up residents and drop off groceries and newspapers. Three diesel cars leave Fort Bragg daily during the summer months, and only one leaves in the winter. The Super Skunk, in operation in the summer, is powered by a steam locomotive almost half a century old. It makes only one stop between Fort Bragg and Willits.

For a timetable and reservations write to Reservation Desk, California Western Railroad, Fort Bragg, California 95437. Round trip fare is $4.50 for adults ($3.00 one way) and half fare for children 5 through 11. Children under 5 ride free if they do not occupy a separate seat. If you make reservations by mail, you must include the total fare.

The Northwestern Pacific Railroad operates passenger service between Willits and Eureka every day except Tuesday. An air-conditioned diesel rail car leaves Willits each Monday, Thursday, and Saturday at 1:45 P.M. for the 5½ hour trip to Eureka, and leaves Eureka each Sunday, Wednesday, and Friday at 10:05 A.M. for the return trip to Willits.

Like the California Western, the Northwestern Pacific tends to shun the highway. The route follows the Eel River north through dramatic Eel River Canyon, crosses the river three times, and passes through 26 tunnels between Willits and Eureka. Fares are $4.86 one way and $8.75 round trip. Children 5 through 11 ride for half fare. For the under-5 set, the trip is free.

THE REDWOOD HIGHWAY

Before the Gold Rush brought a surge of new population to Northern California, a vast forest of the towering redwood—the *Sequoia sempervirens*—blanketed an area up to 30 miles wide, ranging 450 miles from the Santa Lucia Mountains south of Monterey northward into a corner of Oregon.

The demands of civilization have left only small parts of the primeval forest. But a few of the surviving groves have been set aside for the education and enjoyment of present and future generations. These are located along U.S. 101 from Leggett north to Crescent City. They are one of the great scenic attractions in California, and one unique in the world—for these trees grow in no other region.

Weather

The redwoods are worth a visit (or many visits) whenever it is possible to get there. The finest season is autumn, when the crowds thin out, the air turns brisk, and the seasonal show of color brightens the countryside.

Eureka, the major city in the redwoods, is one of the cooler places in the nation—from June until October. From this city north to the Oregon border, the weather is much the same as on the Mendocino coast. South of Eureka, after U.S. 101 cuts over behind the coast hills, you get an entirely different kind of climate. The mountains screen out the cooling ocean air; as a result summers are warm and dry.

PUFFING across bridge over Noyo River, Super Skunk travels through redwoods between Fort Bragg and Willits.

SOUTH FORK of Eel River winds serenely between redwoods in Humboldt State Park on fall morning.

Accommodations

Much like the Mendocino coast, the redwood country has limited overnight accommodations. There are many more motels and hotels along the highway, but traffic is correspondingly heavier. Eureka and Arcata have a number of fine motels between them, but during summer's tourist peak it is necessary to have advance reservations. Without advance reservations, you will have a better chance of finding a place to stay in Crescent City. Roadside motels and inns are scattered along the road between Willits and Eureka. Ukiah, at the southern extreme of the redwood country, also has a number of hotels and motels.

Richardson Grove State Park

As you enter Humboldt County from the south on U.S. 101 you come to Richardson Grove State Park. Here are swimming holes along the Eel River's South Fork and highly developed campgrounds. You can eat in the restaurant, or buy groceries for use at the camping or picnicking facilities. There are 10 miles of hiking trails, and a ranger conducts trail walks during the summer season. Richardson Grove is open the year around. In the winter silver and king salmon and steelhead trout attract many fishermen.

Humboldt Redwoods State Park

Humboldt Redwoods State Park, scattered along 42 miles of U.S. 101 between Garberville and Pepperwood, begins unobtrusively at the Whittemore Grove across the South Fork Eel River from the highway. To reach it, turn off at Redway on the Briceland Road.

The old shady, two-lane Redwood Highway is paralleled by U.S. 101 through the Humboldt Redwoods area. In several places, you can still drive the old highway, which has been retained as a secondary road now called "Avenue of the Giants."

Beyond Miranda, the South Fork groves are fairly continuous to the junction with the main Eel, with major breaks at Myers Flat, Weott, and the freeway overpass that has cut a tremendous swath between the Founders' and California Federation of Women's Clubs groves. At Burlington, in a dark copse of second growth, an all-year campground adjoins the park headquarters. Rangers on duty will give you information on camping and picnic facilities in other parts of the park and in the fall will tell where to see the best color display.

At Founders' Grove take the Rockefeller Forest offramp from U.S. 101 to the short trail leading to the Founders' Tree. For many years people considered this the world's tallest tree, at 364 feet. A broken top has brought the figure down to 347 feet, and the honors for tallest tree are bestowed upon an unnamed 359-footer at Bull Creek Flat in Rockefeller Forest.

The Founders' Tree, along with thousands of other redwoods, is taller than the tallest of any other species. The loop trail beyond the Founders' Tree is short, but it takes you well into the solemn depths of the forest where delicate living things thrive.

Driving north out of the Founders' Grove on Avenue of the Giants, take a side road to the wide pebble beach of the Eel. Here, instead of being enclosed and overwhelmed by close-up redwoods, you can stand back and look at them from top to bottom. Where firm pebbles show at the traveled surface, you can drive safely on the beach, but don't venture onto the sand or loose gravel areas.

A side trip to the Bull Creek flats will be a highlight of your trip into the redwoods despite recent damage that has reduced the forest from 500 acres to 435 acres today. Logging runoff from an unprecedented heavy rainfall brought down debris that raised the bed of Bull Creek fully five feet, forcing the stream to swing widely from side to side and cut far back into its banks. More than 600 of the big redwoods, undermined by the stream, have fallen. The state has taken preventive measures to avoid more damage arising from the Bull Creek watershed.

From the main road through the Rockefeller Forest, you can take a narrow road down toward Bull Creek and the site of the present "tallest" tree, "Giant" tree and "Flatiron" tree.

If you want to spend some time along the Eel River, cross the fords and foot-bridges to the solitude of the Children's Forest, Canoe Creek basin with its superb Garden Clubs of America Grove, and other virgin park lands across the river.

Ferndale

Just west of the Redwood Highway (take the Fernbridge exit off U.S. 101), is Ferndale, a Victorian village with all of the old-fashioned charm of Mendocino. As you approach Ferndale you pass herds of cattle in fenced pastures around big, weathered barns. Main Street, which curves into town, has many picturesque buildings, painted effectively to accent the elaborate displays of carpenter Gothic.

Ferndale hosts two fairs yearly—the county fair in August and an art festival in May. Art exhibits line Main Street and sidewalk cafes or refreshment stands are set up among them. Flowers are prominent.

Outdoor activities include trout fishing at Francis Creek, Williams Creek, and Reas Creek. These creeks are part of the Junior Fishing Reserves and only boys and girls 14 and under are allowed to fish these waters. For a steep uphill climb, then some good high views, try 30-acre Russ Park. The only entrance is a primitive road which soon becomes a trail. Take Ocean Avenue ⅔ mile east from Main Street; go uphill just west of the Catholic cemetery.

SALT MARSHES on Humboldt Bay's Gunther Island provide food and shelter for about 30 species of birds.

Humboldt Bay

Isolated from the noisy bustle of downtown Eureka by a narrow channel of water, Gunther Island is easily accessible by boat and is one of the last unspoiled places left on Humboldt Bay. On the island you can watch nesting egrets, dig in the mud for clams, or picnic on a grassy knoll.

You can still dig clams as the Indians did along the muddy shores of the island. The minus tides at the end of June and the beginning and end of July make for good clamming. To dig the geoducks, gapers, and Martha Washingtons from the goo, you only need a shovel, old clothes, and a little luck. These clams are safe to eat all year, but between May and September remove all the dark parts before preparing them, since they may contain toxic residue.

The crossing from Eureka to the island is short and can be made pleasantly in a dinghy or rowboat. You can launch your boat from the ramp at the foot of Commercial Street, or rental boats are available.

Before going to Gunther Island, it is necessary to obtain a permit from the city manager's office at the Eureka city hall (the office is open weekdays only).

Fort Humboldt State Historical Monument

A selection of equipment used for logging at the turn of the century is on display at Fort Humboldt State Historical Monument. You can see axes, saws, and wedges, the personal tools of yesterday's lumberjack,

RUGGED SHORE of Trinidad State Beach is typical of northern coast; cove here is protected from wind.

near a reconstruction of a typical logger's cabin. Close by are some of the heavy steam engines used to handle the logs.

The exhibit, just a half mile off U.S. 101 on the southern edge of Eureka, is open daily from dawn to dusk. Behind the park headquarters is a small museum that gives a brief history of the original fort, constructed in the 1850's and abandoned in 1865. U. S. Grant was one of the soldiers stationed here.

Beach Parks near Eureka

Although not actually in the redwoods, the four state parks along the coast just north of Eureka make delightful stopping places as you drive the Redwood Highway north toward the Oregon border. Only Patrick's Point State Park has camping facilities, but you can picnic at any of the parks.

Little River State Beach is a shallow, sandy beach. It's a good place to dig for razor clams, which are buried at the tide line (no closed season, but a fishing license is required).

Trinidad State Beach is 4 miles north of Little River. The cove here is nicely sheltered from the wind.

Patrick's Point State Park, 23 miles north of Eureka in a California "rain forest," has complete camping and picnicking facilities. A canopy of big old firs, pines, cypresses, alders, and Sitka spruce shades a

thick undergrowth of salal, bracken, and other native plants. So dense is the native growth that it screens the campsites and makes them pleasantly private. Paved roads lead to various parts of the park, and several trails invade the seclusion of the forest and then emerge on the bluff above the sea.

Dry Lagoon State Park near Orick is used mostly by fishermen, but it, too, is a fine spot for a picnic.

REDWOOD NATIONAL PARK

A representative segment of old growth redwood and the outstanding coastal scenery in Northern California are now being protected so that generations from now, people will be able to witness the magnificent trees and the plant and animal life which they nurture. Authorized in 1968, Redwood National Park is 46 miles long (extending from Crescent City south to a point on Redwood Creek opposite Big Lagoon) and 7 miles wide at its greatest width.

At the southern end of the park are Lady Bird Grove and Tall Trees Grove. Lady Bird Grove is located along the Bald Hills Road two miles east of U.S. 101 (just north of Orick). A ½ mile trail will take you to the site where Mrs. Lyndon Johnson dedicated the national park on November 25, 1968. Tall Trees Grove can be reached by an 8½ mile trail (17 miles round trip) which begins at a point along Redwood Creek just west of the Bald Hills Road near Arcata Redwood Company's Mill A. Two small back country campsites are located on the creek bank along the way. Fires are permitted only at these two sites.

Three state parks (Prairie Creek, Del Norte, and Jedediah Smith) offering trails, streams, herds of elk, beaches, and fine campsites are included within the boundaries of Redwood National Park. As funds are available the national park will develop its own trails, interpretive facilities, and campsites. National Park Service information centers are located at Orick, Klamath, and Crescent City.

Prairie Creek Redwoods State Park

Anyone who has camped at Prairie Creek is likely to love it best of all the redwood parks. It does have more than its share of special wonders, two of which are the beautiful creek itself, and the broad expanse of meadow where you can observe the herd of native Roosevelt elk that stays here most of the time.

Prairie Creek has rain-forest overtones. You encounter luxuriant mosses and lichens; five-fingered ferns grow profusely and cover Fern Canyon's 50-foot-high walls. Besides the redwood and Douglas fir, you will see western hemlock, lowland fir, and Sitka spruce. Although about 100 inches of rain falls on Prairie Creek most years, high ground to the west protects it from most of the chilly ocean winds and fog.

You can best see Prairie Creek Park by hiking on some of its 21 trails. Ten begin at the park headquarters where there is a trail map. Two campgrounds, Prairie Creek and Gold Bluffs Beach, offer a total of 100 sites.

Three miles south of the park entrance on U.S. 101 a side road marked Davison's Dairy will take you to the wild shores of Gold Bluffs. Follow this road for 12 miles past the dairy through cut-over land to the ocean shore. From this point, a broad, flat strand backed up by picturesque cliffs stretches north for more than 8 miles. If you are a surf angler or a glass-float collector, here is a happy hunting ground.

Del Norte Coast Redwoods State Park

In Del Norte Coast Redwoods State Park, you enjoy both a drive through rugged inland forest on two-lane U.S. 101 and vistas of the rugged Pacific shore from high turnouts south of the wooded section. Damnation Creek Trail will take you on foot through the dense forest to the ocean, where there are tidepools and giant redwoods grow almost at the ocean's edge.

Del Norte has excellent camping facilities at Mill Creek Campground, 1 mile east of U.S. 101. Mill Creek runs through the camp and provides swimming, wading, and trout fishing during the season.

Jedediah Smith Redwoods State Park

Northeast of Crescent City on U.S. Highway 199 is Jedediah Smith Redwoods State Park. At the northernmost end of the Redwood National Park, Jedediah Smith presents the rare spectacle of a skyline ridge still tightly furred with giant redwoods. The highway runs through the hilly Tyson Grove and the National Tribute Grove (just two of 10 memorial groves in the park) and then out onto a magnificent flat, where some of the most imposing redwoods of all stand among loose growths of vine maple, salal, Oregon grape, and ferns.

Paralleling Mill Creek through the park is the longest non-streamlined road (almost 5 miles) in the redwoods. The Howland Hill Road is very narrow and unpaved, but it has a well-packed-gravel base that makes for secure driving even after the fall rains. If you take this road, you will be following the original stage route here, and if you know where to look, you can see remains of the old split-log road that carried travelers over a century ago.

The Smith River provides good salmon, steelhead, and trout fishing in season, and sandy beaches for sun bathing. Jedediah Smith provides numerous campsites and trails. One hiking trail goes to Stout Grove, where redwoods are over 300 feet tall; another crosses a rustic bridge and winds through dense redwood to end at the abandoned Nickerson Ranch.

GIANT TREES flank entrance to Lady Bird Grove in Redwood National Park. A ½-mile trail leads to grove.

SOUTH FROM SAN FRANCISCO

Peninsula Cities • Beaches • State Parks • San Juan Bautista

Stanford University

The narrow belt of land south of San Francisco is divided into two distinctly different regions by a forested ridge of mountains that runs down its length. The bay side of the mountains is crowded with cities, while the ocean side is sprinkled with peaceful farms, unspoiled beaches, and lightly-traveled country roads.

Palo Alto is the end of the peninsula proper. But generally the cities of Mountain View, Los Altos, Sunnyvale, Santa Clara, and San Jose are considered as part of this region. This area at the southern tip of the bay is the scene of heavy industry. Moffett Naval Air Station is located here, along with many electronics and chemical firms and a variety of large and small businesses.

There are several main routes down the peninsula from San Francisco. State Highway 1 skirts the coast, Skyline Boulevard (State Highway 35) follows the ridge of the mountains, and Junipero Serra Freeway (Interstate 280) runs along the east side of the mountain spine. The Bayshore Freeway (U.S. Highway 101) and El Camino Real (State Highway 82) go through the population centers that edge the bay.

The Santa Cruz Highway (State Highway 17) offers a delightful, easy-to-drive connecting route from the southern end of the bay across the Santa Cruz mountains to the coast. The highway climbs in long, sweeping curves through beautifully wooded slopes. Traffic is generally light, except on summer weekends when cars head toward the cool coastal areas and the popular beach parks around Santa Cruz.

A more northerly cross-peninsula route, State Highway 84, leaves Bayshore Freeway (or El Camino Real) at Belmont and reaches the coast at Half Moon Bay. It intersects Skyline Boulevard at Crystal Springs Reservoir.

ALONG THE BAY SHORE

Originally, the peninsula cities grew as suburbs of San Francisco; but in recent years the ideal climate and pleasant living conditions of the area have attracted industry, business, and an ever-increasing residential population that works where it lives—on the peninsula.

Two main highways lead south from San Francisco through these urban areas. You can drive from San Francisco to the southern tip of the bay without encountering a stop light. Bayshore is not a scenic route —much of the time it consists of bleak views of the bay and uninspiring subdivisions.

Rock bridge near Santa Cruz

Lick Observatory atop Mt. Hamilton

El Camino Real roughly parallels Bayshore Freeway all the way to San Jose. But where the freeway skirts along the edge of the bay, El Camino slowly passes through the towns. This is the route to take if you want a sampling of the peninsula's cities, commercial and residential areas. The Bayshore Freeway and El Camino Real are but a short distance apart, and frequently there is a connecting road.

Candlestick Park

As you leave San Francisco on the Bayshore Freeway you can glimpse Candlestick Park stadium on Candlestick Point. The stadium is in use almost the year around with the San Francisco Giants playing baseball from mid-April to late September and the San Francisco 49ers playing football from September to December.

The Cow Palace

The huge sports arena, on Geneva Avenue in San Mateo County, is reached by turning off Bayshore Freeway at Third Street. This is the site of the Grand National livestock exposition, horse show, and rodeo,

a very popular event which draws large crowds of spectators every fall. Also held at the Cow Palace are basketball games, circuses, prize fights, and occasional big conventions.

San Francisco International Airport

From Bayshore Freeway near San Bruno, you can see busy San Francisco International Airport, spreading along the edge of the bay east of the highway.

Two terminal buildings accommodate the 15 million air travelers that pass through the airport annually. The seven-story Central Terminal Building has restaurants, lounges, shops, and an observation deck. The South Terminal Building, an 800-foot sweeping arc structure, also provides passenger service facilities. A $141 million expansion program is underway to provide modern accommodations for the anticipated growth in air passenger traffic.

Exclusive residential areas

A short side trip into Hillsborough, in the hills south and west of Burlingame, will take you through beautiful grounds and palatial homes. Atherton, south of

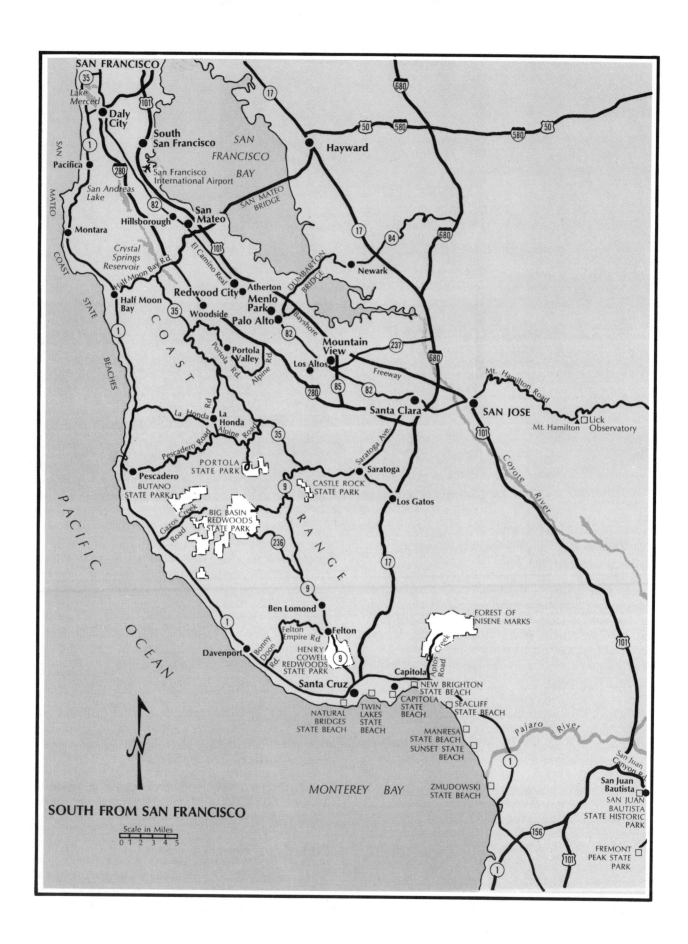

SOUTH FROM SAN FRANCISCO

BEAR AND CUBS is one of Benny Bufano sculptures in mall area of Hillsdale Shopping Center in San Mateo.

BOAT LEAVES from Harbor Island for half-hour guided tour of waterways and islands of Marine World.

Redwood City, is another area of large estates. It is heavily wooded, and a drive down one of its roads will quickly show the natural beauty and feeling of seclusion that give this region its appeal.

Woodside is an area of fine homes with more of a rural look. Many of the residents own horses, and riding trails and pasture land are an integral part of the community. The center of town, reached via Woodside Road west of El Camino Real, is actually quite small—little more than a village. The old one-room Woodside Store, built in 1854, is open as a county museum (Wednesday through Saturday 10 A.M. to 12 noon, 1 to 5 P.M.; Sunday 1 to 5 P.M.). South of Woodside are many interesting homes in the hills of Portola Valley.

Marine World

Marine World is located on a 60-acre stretch of tidal flats east of the Bayshore Freeway in Redwood City. To reach this water wonderland follow the Ralston Avenue exit off the Bayshore to Marine World Parkway. Marine World is open Wednesday through Sunday from 9:30 A.M. to 6:30 P.M. Admission is $3.50 for adults (18 and over); $2.50 for juniors (12-17); and $1.50 for children (6-11). Children five and under are admitted free if accompanied by a parent.

Several islands connected by waterways and bridges make up Marine World. At Harbor Island there is an information booth, a restaurant, and some marine specialty shops. This island is the launching site for a boat tour around the complex.

Across Seal Rock Cove is Oceanarium Island, where a killer whale, dolphins, and sea lions perform at Oceana Theater. You can glimpse exotic marine life on the floor of Nautilus Reef, reached through a glass-enclosed elevator which descends to the ocean bottom. There is also an open aquarium where children are able to get a close look at small sea creatures.

On Olympic Island, an hour-long show at the Marine Stadium features exciting boat races and water-skiing exhibitions.

Sunset offices and gardens

In Menlo Park, visitors are welcome at the editorial and business offices of *Sunset* Magazine and *Sunset* Books. The two buildings are located at Willow and Middlefield roads (between Bayshore Freeway and El Camino Real). Hostesses are on hand Monday through Friday to take visitors on conducted tours at 10:30 and 11:30 A.M., 1, 2, and 3 P.M. You will see the kitchen where all recipes are tested before they are published; and you can stroll through the

PALM DRIVE, main entrance to Stanford, leads to heart of campus—the 17-acre Quadrangle. Behind the native sandstone buildings rise the foothills. Note Memorial Church in center.

extensive demonstration gardens of outstanding trees, shrubs, and flowers native to all sections of the Pacific Coast from the Northwest to Mexico. Plantings are changed frequently, and the gardens are colorful at any time of year.

Allied Arts Guild

A visit to the Allied Arts Guild in Menlo Park (Arbor Road at Creek Drive) offers a glimpse of the early, more leisurely Spanish California. The 3½-acre site that the Guild occupies is part of the once vast Spanish land grant, El Rancho de las Pulgas (Ranch of the Fleas). The original barn and sheep sheds of the old ranch still stand and now house the shops of craftsmen. The new buildings housing a variety of shops preserve the Spanish Colonial theme of the original ranch. The Guild is operated by the Woodside-Atherton Auxiliary for the benefit of the Stanford Children's Convalescent Hospital and is open to visitors daily except Sunday from 9:30 A.M. until 5 P.M. In the dining room, luncheon and tea are served. Reservations are advisable.

Palo Alto

Palo Alto developed as an outgrowth of Stanford University and took its name from a local landmark, *El Palo Alto*. This tall redwood, where Spanish explorers led by Gaspar de Portola camped in 1769, is located where Alma Street crosses the railroad tracks next to San Francisquito Creek, the boundary between Palo Alto and Menlo Park. It can best be seen by driving north on El Camino Real and glancing back to your right after you pass the Stanford Shopping Center.

Palo Alto is a well-planned city of 56,000 with many parks, five libraries, two community centers, and a junior museum.

Baylands Nature Interpretive Center, at 2775 Embarcadero, provides a focal point for the study of San Francisco Bay. With facilities for housing exhibits, small laboratories for microscopic study of the bay, meeting rooms for local conservationists, a salt water aquarium, and a boardwalk to walk out on the marsh, the Center is open to the public from 12 noon to 5 P.M. Monday through Friday and 10 A.M. to 5

P.M. on weekends. Slide talks and lectures are offered.

Nearby is the city's golf course and the 12-acre Baylands Athletic Center with two lighted ball diamonds and a 500-seat enclosed grandstand.

Palo Alto's Junior Museum, at 1451 Middlefield Road, is connected to an outdoor live zoo that features animals indigenous to the area, like bobcats, eagles, and raccoons. The museum is open from 10 A.M. to 5 P.M. Tuesday through Friday, from 9 A.M. to 5 P.M. Saturday, and from 1 to 4 P.M. Sunday.

Lucy Stern Community Center, at 1305 Middlefield Road, houses the Palo Alto Community Theater and Children's Theater as well as several auditoriums for folk and modern dancing, and meeting rooms. Behind the center and extending to Newell Road is Rinconada Park, a 19-acre facility with lighted tennis courts, picnic facilities, and a large swimming pool.

The new Mitchell Park Community Center, at 3700 Middlefield, has a youth center, a large social hall, and four activity rooms, including a ceramics workshop area and kiln.

Stanford University

University Avenue, Palo Alto's main business street, crosses El Camino Real on an overpass southeast of Menlo Park. West of El Camino Real, it becomes Palm Drive, the palm-lined approach to Stanford University.

At the entrance of the Quadrangle at the end of Palm Drive, the Stanford Guide Service Information Center has an assortment of maps (one of which outlines a tour of the campus) and descriptive material. The center is open daily from 10 A.M. to 5 P.M. Guided tours leave daily at 2 P.M.

An easily visible campus landmark is the 285-foot tower of the Hoover Institution of War, Revolution, and Peace. An elevator goes to the top where you get a visual orientation of the campus. Hoover Tower is open from 10 A.M. to 5 P.M. Monday through Saturday, 12 noon to 5 P.M. Sunday.

You will want to see the Memorial Church, dedicated in 1903 and completely rebuilt after the 1906 earthquake. The large cruciform church is decorated with Venetian mosaics, most striking of which are reproductions of "The Sermon on the Mount" on the front facade and Rosselli's "Last Supper" in the chancel. Except when services are in progress, the church is open to visitors from 10 A.M. to 5 P.M. daily.

Across Panama Street south of the Memorial Church are White Memorial Plaza and Tresidder Memorial Union. Both are handsome examples of the "new" campus now completed or in construction. A free-form fountain is the focal point of the plaza.

Northwest of the general campus buildings, on Quarry Road, is the Stanford University Medical Center. It is best known for its pioneering work in the development of uses of the atom for treatment of cancer, basic techniques of heart transplantation, and programs for understanding basic causes of mental retardation. A tour of the Medical Center leaves daily at 3 P.M. from the information desk in the hospital lobby.

METROPOLITAN SAN JOSE AREA

Spreading out from the tip of San Francisco Bay, the Metropolitan San Jose area has undergone an industrial explosion which transformed the northern section of the Santa Clara Valley from an agricultural region to a big manufacturing center. Small semi-rural communities have expanded into side-by-side urban areas. The San Jose region is composed of a multitude of housing subdivisions and many industrial parks; however, there are also some interesting attractions which are well worth your while to visit.

San Jose

One of the nation's fastest-growing cities, San Jose originally began in 1777 with a population of 66. It remained a small town, taking a back seat to the famous city farther north, until the early 1950's when industry moved in and opened up the area. Although many orchards were removed to provide housing for the growing population, San Jose is still a major canning and fruit-drying center.

One of the city's most popular attractions is the San Jose Zoological Gardens at Kelly Park. Almost one hundred animals are on view in 14 exhibit areas at the 2-acre zoo. Besides lions, jaguars, and seals, you can see such exotic animals as Malayan sun bears,

HAPPY HOLLOW, a playground in San Jose's Kelly Park, delights youngsters with boat displays.

caymans, and emus. One of the best exhibits, with both above-water and under-water views, is the river otter section. The zoo is open daily except Monday from 11 A.M. to 6 P.M. during the summer; from 11 A.M. to 4:30 P.M. during the winter. To reach the zoo, take the Story Road exit off the Bayshore Freeway (U.S. 101) and continue four blocks south.

Also at Kelly Park are the Municipal Japanese Tea Garden and a children's playground. Happy Hollow, which features a steamboat, a treehouse, and puppet shows, is open from 11 A.M. to 6 P.M. daily from mid-June to September 10; Saturday and Sunday only from September 11 to December 31 and from Easter to mid-June. The playground is closed from January to Easter.

Another San Jose attraction is the Winchester Mystery House, four miles west of the city via the Santa Clara-Los Gatos Highway. Sarah Winchester, heir to her father-in-law's gun fortune, was an eccentric who believed that if she stopped adding rooms onto her house she would die. The 160-room house is practically devoid of furniture as all the household furnishings were removed after Mrs. Winchester's death in 1922. There are frequent tours of the Mystery House, which is open from 9 A.M. to 4 P.M. Monday through Friday; 9 A.M. to 4:30 P.M. Saturday and Sunday. Admission is $1.50 for those 12 and older, 30 cents for children 6-11.

Other attractions in San Jose are the 5½-acre Municipal Rose Garden at Naglee and Dana Avenues; San Jose State College at 125 South Seventh Street; Alum Rock Park at the end of Alum Rock Road in the foothills; Egyptian temple museum, a library, and a planetarium at Rosicrucian Park at 1342 Naglee Avenue; and Frontier Village, just south of the city limits on Monterey Road.

Mount Hamilton and Lick Observatory

Twenty miles southeast of San Jose, the University of California's Lick Observatory is reached by a winding, narrow road that climbs to the summit of 4,209-foot Mount Hamilton.

As you climb over three ridges of the Coast Range, you drive through peaceful country where cattle graze in lush meadows and weathered fences follow the contours of the hills as far as the eye can see. As you climb the second ridge, you will see the dome of the observatory glistening in the sun.

BUSINESS TOURS ON THE PENINSULA

Many factories, government offices, and industries offer free tours to visitors. Some require advance notice, but others are available at any time. Here is just a sample of the variety you will find:

• Syntex Laboratory and Research Center. Groups may visit Syntex, located in Stanford's Industrial Park at 3401 Hillview Avenue, Palo Alto, on Wednesday from 2 to 4 p.m. by appointment only. A special attraction is a fine collection of contemporary art, including Henry Moore's Seated Woman.

• Leslie Salt. Located on Harbor Blvd. in Redwood City, Leslie Salt offers tours for groups of eight or more from October through early December. You must make arrangements 2 weeks in advance.

• Ampex. Also in Redwood City at 411 Broadway, Ampex offers a half-hour slide lecture and two-hour tour of its electronics plant on Wednesday from 9:30 to 11:30 a.m. Advance reservations are required.

• Safe-T-Pacific. Groups of 10 to 30 can arrange for a half-hour tour of this ice cream cone plant. The building is located at 2500 Middlefield Road in Redwood City.

• Stanford Linear Accelerator Center. If you call several weeks in advance, you can arrange to tour Stanford University's two-mile-long electron accelerator. A 90-minute tour, designed mainly for scientific groups, includes a bus ride around the 480-acre center.

• U.S. Geological Survey. Tours are offered once a month at 2 p.m. and every three months at 7:30 p.m.; call ahead for an appointment. The tour includes a look at map-making procedures at the survey's headquarters at 345 Middlefield Road in Menlo Park.

• Moffett Field. Tours are scheduled at 9:30 a.m. and 1:30 p.m. Tuesday through Friday, but written arrangements are required three weeks in advance. A two-hour tour of the Naval Air Station is offered to anyone over 12.

• Frito-Lay. Located at 650 N. King Road in San Jose, this potato chip plant offers tours Tuesday, Wednesday, and Thursday between 9 a.m. and 2 p.m. These tours are unusually popular, so call in advance.

• Spice Islands. Tours, which include a free sample and recipes, are offered either Tuesday or Thursday at 10:30 a.m. or 2:30 p.m. at 100 E. Grand Avenue in South San Francisco. Arrangements must be made in advance. You may visit the test kitchens, quality control lab, and see the complete refining process. Children under 14 are not permitted.

Visitors are welcome at the observatory every Saturday and Sunday (except national and university holidays) from 1 to 5 P.M. There is no admission charge, and guide service is provided. Of particular interest is the 120-inch reflector telescope (second largest in the world) which you can view from a small gallery in the dome where it is housed.

Mission Santa Clara de Asis

Eighth in the chain of California missions, Santa Clara de Asis was founded in 1777 along the banks of the Guadalupe River. The mission had several locations and structures, until the present site was selected and the church constructed in 1825. One hundred years later fire practically destroyed the mission; however, in 1929 a concrete replica was completed.

A cross, dating back to 1777, stands in a protective covering of redwood in front of the church. In the belltower, a bell given by the King of Spain in 1778 still tolls. Above a side altar inside the church is a magnificent crucifix which survived the 1926 fire.

Mission Santa Clara, transferred from the Franciscans to the Jesuits in 1851, is part of the campus of the University of Santa Clara. This co-educational Catholic school is located on The Alameda in Santa Clara. You can visit the mission daily.

Los Gatos

The small foothill town of Los Gatos has undergone some changes recently that make it a popular shopping stop. Also here are parks for picnics, charming old residences, and a winery to tour. To reach Los Gatos, take the State 17 turnoff southwest from the Bayshore Freeway (U.S. 101) in San Jose.

The best-known attraction is Old Town, a lively collection of shops, artists' studios, restaurants, and theaters housed in a converted elementary school. Most stores in Old Town are open Tuesday through Sunday from 10 A.M. to 9 P.M.; most of the restaurants serve lunch and dinner daily. To reach Old Town leave State 17 at Saratoga Avenue. Turn left on University Avenue and in about half a mile you're there.

On three sides of Old Town is a growing collection of used-furniture and antique stores. Walk along Santa Cruz Avenue, then turn onto Main Street and you see the 2-block stretch where most of the stores are located. Across the Main Street freeway overpass is a handsomely restored gift store and an emporium of used furniture.

Four blocks from Old Town, Burnham House, a small modern art gallery in a remodeled Victorian-era home, presents a schedule of shows, frequently featuring local artists. You will find the gallery at 45 Broadway (off Santa Cruz Avenue). It is open Tues-

OLD TOWN in Los Gatos is former schoolhouse turned into collection of small shops, studios, restaurants.

day through Friday from 1:30 to 5 P.M.; Saturday and Sunday from 11 A.M. to 5 P.M.

Picnicking families should head for the two expansive parks that sprawl side by side across the north end of the town. On a sunny weekend, the lake in Vasona Park is filled with fluttering sails. You can rent sailboats at $3 to $7 an hour or rowboats for $2.50 at this county park. Fishermen will find crappie, bass, and catfish in the lake and a pier and unobstructed shoreline to fish from. Fishing continues the year around. To get to Vasona Park, take the Lark Avenue exit off State 17; the park entrance is west of the freeway, just off Lark. The adjoining Oak Meadow Park has an 18-inch narrow-gauge steamer locomotive and a turn-of-the-century station for waiting passengers.

Los Gatos is filled with examples of "carpenter Gothic"—houses decorated with fretwork, medallions, and stained glass—dating back as much as 85 years. One of the richest areas for old-house fanciers is between Pennsylvania and Hernandez avenues. Another good area is Fairview Avenue (which leads off Pennsylvania) and around the small cul-de-sac park in the middle of Fairview Plaza.

You can do some wine touring at Novitiate Winery, which produces sacramental wine for much of the Jesuit order and in addition sells aperitif, dessert, and a limited number of table wines. Tours of the hillside winery take place every Tuesday and Friday from 2 to 3 P.M. You can taste and buy wine every day except Sunday from 9 to 11 A.M. and 2 to 4 P.M. From Main turn towards the mountains on College Avenue, which leads to Prospect Avenue and the Novitiate.

Saratoga's attractions

Tucked into the hills just behind the town of Saratoga is an unexpected bit of the Orient. Formerly a private garden established in 1917, Hakone Gardens is now a city park, open free of charge daily from 10 A.M. to dusk. This 2-acre garden contains hundreds of Japanese plants and a teahouse, where tea is usually served midday. From Stevens Creek Freeway (State Highway 85) follow Saratoga-Sunnyvale Road to Saratoga and the junction with Big Basin Way. Hakone Gardens is less than a mile beyond.

The Paul Masson Champagne Cellars, at 13150 Saratoga Avenue, welcomes visitors daily from 10 A.M. to 4 P.M. Most of Paul Masson's vineyards are further south at Pinnacles, but Saratoga is where the wine comes for bottling. After an informative tour, you are welcome to sample wines in their tasting room.

Masson's original winery is the site of "Music in the Vineyards." On weekends in July and August, chamber groups and soloists appear in afternoon programs with an intermission for champagne. Tickets for the concert are $3.50. To be on the concert mailing list and to order tickets, write Music at the Vineyards, 330 Jackson Street, San Francisco 94111.

Side trips south on U.S. 101

If you follow U.S. Highway 101 south from San Jose you can explore an old mission town, stroll through floral growing grounds, or picnic or camp off-the-beaten-track at Fremont Peak State Park.

About 40 miles south of San Jose on State Highway

BRACKET BRIDGE, in Saratoga's Hakone Gardens, arches over clear pond where children look for goldfish.

156, just 3½ miles off U.S. 101, the San Juan Bautista State Historical Monument presents a carefully restored chapter of early California history. Once a crossroads of stagecoach travel, the old mission village declined after the railroad pushed south from San Francisco. However, in 1933 San Juan Bautista became a state historical monument and old San Juan was preserved.

The history of the San Juan Valley centers on the mission, founded by the Franciscan Fathers in 1797. Construction of the present mission building began in 1803 and was completed in 1814. You enter the mission from the long, cloistered colonnade which forms one side of the village plaza. There is no admission charge, but visitors are asked to contribute to the maintenance of the building and gardens.

The state monument properties include the old San Juan Plaza, the Plaza Hotel, the Castro House, the Plaza Stable and blacksmith shed, the Zanetta House (or Old Plaza Hall), the Zanetta Cottage, and a walled orchard behind the old hotel. These buildings are open to the public daily from 8 A.M. to 5 P.M. (8 A.M. to 6 P.M. June through August). Admission charge is 25 cents per adult.

San Juan Bautista also offers several fine restaurants, and once a year vendors display their wares at a bustling Flea Market.

Just east of San Juan Bautista on State 156 are the extensive fields of the Ferry-Morse Seed Company. Visitors are welcome to wander through the flower gardens located near the Headquarters Ranch Buildings. Ferry-Morse is open daily during daylight hours.

Fremont Peak State Park lies 11 miles south of San Juan Bautista via the San Juan Canyon-State Park Road. The park marks the spot where, in 1846, Captain John C. Fremont raised the American flag over California soil.

At this 287-acre park there are picnic tables, campsites, and several nature trails over wooded limestone ridges and through chaparral canyons. A ½-mile hiking trail from the camp area takes you to the 3,169-foot summit of Fremont Peak. From the top, you can look east across the checkerboard farmlands of the San Benito River Valley and west to the crescent shoreline of Monterey Bay.

At Fremont State Park, there is a charge of $2 per night per car for campers; 75 cents a car for picnickers. Firewood is sold at park headquarters for 50 cents a box.

THROUGH THE MOUNTAINS

Skyline Boulevard (State Highway 35) will take you along the mountain spine of the peninsula. (Interstate 280 runs just east of the mountains.) The Santa

PULGAS WATER TEMPLE, along Canada Road, marks end of water pipeline which begins in Yosemite.

Cruz Mountains, a spur of the Coast Range, stretch from the Crystal Springs area down just below Santa Cruz, east of Monterey Bay. Standing 2,000 to 3,000 feet high, these mountains in the winter receive heavy rains which help to produce the forests of Douglas fir, pine, madrone, maple, alder, bay, and the towering, shadowy redwoods that make this a cool and shady retreat.

Here you can revel in the fine mountain scenery and enjoy the thrill of catching a glimpse of the ocean on one side and then switching your glance to a panoramic view of San Francisco Bay on the other.

Crystal Springs Reservoir

Near Hillsborough, Skyline Boulevard and Interstate 280 pass by Crystal Springs Reservoir which holds the water supply for San Francisco. Toward the southern end of the reservoir, Skyline Boulevard intersects Canada Road (*Can-YA-da*), a link to Woodside and other residential areas.

INTERSTATE 280 arches high near Crystal Springs. This freeway stretch has won awards for design.

If you take Canada Road, you will see the Pulgas Water Temple at the southern tip of the reservoir. The temple marks the end of the Hetch Hetchy aqueduct, a 162-mile pipeline that begins at an impoundment on the Tuolumne River in the northern section of Yosemite National Park. Around the temple are grounds for picnicking and paths for strolling. Peer into the temple well to see the waters of the Tuolumne surging past. Look to the top of the columns and read the words from Isaiah inscribed there: "I give waters in the wilderness and rivers in the desert to give drink to my people."

Kings Mountain Road and Huddart Park

Some 25 miles south of San Francisco, Skyline Boulevard intersects Kings Mountain Road, a winding, 5-mile route to Woodside. About 2 miles east of Skyline Boulevard on Kings Mountain Road, 970-acre San Mateo County Huddart Park is a good place for a picnic. There are nature trails through the redwoods and madrones, a horse-training ring, horseshoe pitching, an area for volleyball and softball, and general campsites. Entrance fee for picnicking is 50 cents per car and $2 per night for camping.

San Mateo County Memorial Park

The La Honda Road is a link between Skyline Boulevard and San Gregorio near the coast and will take you to San Mateo County Memorial Park (you swing south on Pescadero Road just beyond La Honda). The park has hiking trails, space for baseball games and horseshoe pitching, picnic and barbecue facilities, and 144 campsites. Entrance fee for day use is 50 cents per car and $3 per night for camping.

Portola State Park

Seven miles farther south on Skyline Boulevard is the turnoff to Portola State Park. Follow State 35 south for 7 miles and then turn west on Alpine Road. Here in a deep canyon you can fish, swim, hike, or camp in sites shaded by redwoods, Douglas fir and coast live oak.

San Lorenzo Valley

Where Skyline Boulevard meets Saratoga Gap, a left turn on State Highway 9 will take you to Saratoga, or you can turn right and take State 9 through the San Lorenzo Valley to the coast, where it meets the Coast Highway (State 1) at Santa Cruz.

The shady, wooded San Lorenzo Valley in the Santa Cruz Mountains offers rich fare for the auto explorer. In the valley and the land that flanks it, you will see 100-year-old vineyards, lovely mountain streams, handsome ranches, and orchards. You will wind through groves of giant redwoods and along roads where the evergreen madrones reach across and shut out the sky.

The San Lorenzo River starts near the junction of Skyline Boulevard and State 9 and cuts a crooked course diagonally across the west slope of the Coast Range. It empties into the sea at Santa Cruz. State 9 follows the river all the way and is the "main street" of the valley. Most of the valley's resorts are along this road.

Big Basin Redwoods State Park

The first preserve of redwoods ever set aside as a state park (in 1902), Big Basin Redwoods State Park today is one of the most visited forest parks in California. The Big Basin junction is about 6 miles down State 9 from Skyline Boulevard. Just past the junction, you wind through a leafy tunnel where the madrones reach their red-barked limbs all the way across the road. It is 8 miles from the junction to the park entrance.

In the park you will find some magnificent stands of redwoods, about 35 miles of hiking trails, picnic sites, campgrounds (subject to reservation), and a couple of streams where children can wade. In the summer, planned recreation includes guided nature hikes and a campfire program. The nature lodge, open the year around, contains excellent exhibits of plants and animals of the area.

Horseback riding is permitted on the outer fire roads, but there are no provisions for horses at campsites. Dogs are permitted overnight but must be kept inside an enclosed vehicle or tent; in the daytime they must be kept on a leash.

A trail has recently been completed connecting Big Basin with the new and undeveloped Castle Rock State Park, just south of the junction of State Highways 35 and 9.

Eagle Rock Lookout

On the road from Big Basin to Boulder Creek (State Highway 236), watch for the Jamison Creek Road. It climbs out of the valley in a series of steep switchbacks to the top of Ben Lomond Mountain. At the top keep to the right and you will drive into the scenic setting of the Locatelli Ranch. Follow the dirt road through the ranch to the State Forestry Lookout Station perched on top of Eagle Rock, a 2,488-foot crag. From the lookout station, you can see west to the ocean, north toward Big Basin, and east and south into the San Lorenzo Valley.

BIG BASIN REDWOODS State Park has picnicking sites, campgrounds among magnificent stands of trees.

Along the Empire Grade

From Eagle Rock you may head south along the ridge of Ben Lomond Mountain. You will be driving on the Empire Grade, built in 1872 by farmers working out their poll tax, and named for the Empire Mining Company located near Bonny Doon.

There are two roads that tie the Empire Grade to State 9: the Alba Road that comes in near Ben Lomond, and the Felton Empire Road. Both follow steep, narrow valleys down the east slope of Ben Lomond Mountain.

For a look at the west side of Ben Lomond Mountain, turn off at the Bonny Doon-Pine Flat Road—3½ miles from the north end of the Empire Grade. For a look at the ocean, go 2 miles on the Pine Flat Road and turn right on Ocean View Avenue. This route takes you through another big grove of madrone trees with branches stretching across the road. The country here is more open than in the inland valleys. There are many small ranches with orchards, vineyards, and open rolling grasslands. Look across the pastures and through the trees for views of the ocean.

Ocean View Avenue leads to Bonny Doon, once a lumber town and now a crossroads store surrounded by apple orchards. From here you may head down the hill to Davenport on the coast, angle southeast down Smith Grade to the Empire Grade, or head

OLD-FASHIONED hayride in freight wagon pulled by horses winds through redwoods near Roaring Camp.

CREEK TRAIL in Butano State Park takes you through one of lower stretches of lush redwood forest.

north about a mile and a half and take the Ice Cream Grade and Felton Empire Road back to Felton in the San Lorenzo Valley. The Ice Cream Grade was so named because local residents raised funds for its construction by sponsoring ice cream socials.

Roaring Camp and Big Trees Narrow-Gauge Railroad

One-half mile south of Felton you can board a steam train at a quaint old depot for a 5-mile loop trip through thick redwood groves. If you wish, you can stop over at Bear Mountain for picnicking and hiking and return on a later train.

Roaring Camp offers picnic sites, trout fishing, a full-scale replica of a covered bridge, a general store dating back to the 1880's, and an old-fashioned caboose turned restaurant. Here you can also take a ride in a freight wagon pulled by horses.

Steam passenger trains leave Felton daily at 11 A.M., 12 noon, and 1, 2, 3, and 4 P.M. Roundtrip fare is $2.80 for adults, $1.40 for children 5 to 15 years. There is no charge for youngsters under five.

Henry Cowell Redwoods State Park

A large redwood sign on Highway 9 just south of Felton marks the entrance to this 1,737-acre preserve. The park is a delightful place to spend an hour or more strolling through the trees or following the trails along the San Lorenzo River.

A pleasant picnic area (tables, fireplaces, water) is located along the entrance road, just outside the grove of big trees. A broad, well-drained trail enters the grove of redwoods just south of the picnic area and loops about a mile. Twenty of the larger and more interesting trees are numbered, and you can pick up a keyed guide sheet at the grove entrance. The Giant Tree, largest in the park, is 285 feet high and 51 feet in circumference.

About halfway around the redwood loop trail, you will see a less-distinct path that leads downhill to the San Lorenzo River below the Southern Pacific railroad trestle. The river cuts a winding canyon through the forested San Lorenzo Valley. On warm, sunny afternoons, children can wade in the shallow water of the river or explore the sweeping gravel bars.

Overnight camping is permitted at Graham Hill Campground, at the park's northern boundary. Take the Graham Hill Road east from Felton.

THE COAST HIGHWAY

The most picturesque route down the peninsula is State Highway 1. This Coast Highway follows the shoreline closely and stays away from the larger cities. You will not make good time on this road, but if you enjoy the ocean, beaches, hills, and wind-swept bluffs, this will be the most enjoyable route.

There are several public beaches along the coast, in various stages of development. The most developed areas are invariably the most crowded.

There is one unpredictable factor about this coast route—the fog that rolls in from the ocean. Sometimes you can see it from San Francisco or peninsula cities as it rolls in over the mountain ridge. On other days, the east side of the peninsula will be sunny and warm, but the minute you reach the top of the mountains, the fog reaches up to you from the other side.

If you continue down the coast as far as Santa Cruz, you can take State 17 back across the mountains and then return to San Francisco by a faster route.

San Mateo Coast State Beaches

Ten parcels of bluff, coastal plain, and beach comprise the San Mateo Coast State Beaches. Although often foggy in the summer, these beaches are popular for strolling, picnicking, sunbathing, shallow wading, and surf and rock fishing. The currents are too dangerous for safe swimming.

All of the beaches can be reached from State 1. North to south they are Thornton, Sharp Park, Montara, Half Moon Bay, San Gregorio, Pomponio, Pescadero, Pebble, Arroyo de los Frijoles, and Ano Nuevo.

Butano State Park

Seven miles from Pescadero Beach you can hike, picnic, or camp at Butano State Park. Easiest access to the park is from State Highway 1: from the north take the Pescadero turnoff; from the south, Gazos Creek turnoff. Then head east and follow the signs.

Three major trails traverse the park's 2,186 acres. The Creek Trail starts ¼ mile below the campground and takes you through one of the lower stretches of lush redwood forest. Outlook Trail, one of the park's most pleasant hikes and perhaps most tiring (it climbs 800 feet in one mile) takes you up the side of a hill covered with dense chaparral and evergreen trees to a spot where you can view Ano Nuevo Island just off the coast. Both trails intercept the Perimeter Trail, a fire road that leads into the dry, exposed chalk rock

MONTARA BEACH, along San Mateo County Coast, is popular for sunbathing, picnicking, fishing.

BEACH AND BOARDWALK at Santa Cruz is extremely popular with Bay Area residents on sunny weekends. Boardwalk offers amusement-type attractions; water is excellent for swimming.

area. The hike is not especially scenic, and much of it is unshaded. However, it can be colorful in spring when large rhododendrons burst into bloom.

Santa Cruz

The town of Santa Cruz, at the north end of Monterey Bay and at the mouth of the San Lorenzo River, is a good base for exploring the beaches along this section of the California coast.

At the Santa Cruz waterfront, you can fish off the long municipal pier, go deep sea fishing, enjoy the ocean beach, or try the attractions and rides of the carnival-like boardwalk.

Seven miles north of Santa Cruz on Highway 17, small fry (and their parents) will enjoy Santa's Village, a make-believe community spreading over 33 wooded acres of Scotts Valley. You'll see Santa's house and his workshop; there's a good chance that Santa himself will be about. Santa's Village is open daily, 10 A.M. to 5 P.M., June 10 through September 8. From September 9 through June 8, hours are 10 A.M. to 5 P.M. weekends and regular school holidays.

Santa Cruz has some fascinating examples of Victorian houses. Mission Hill—site of California's 12th mission, founded in 1791—is where the city began and has the largest concentration of "gingerbread."

At the Reliquary (a small museum) attached to the replica of the mission, you can get a pamphlet of the history of Mission Santa Cruz and the surrounding buildings. Although the scale-model replica is only about half the size of the original mission, it was faithfully duplicated from early sketches after the original was destroyed by earthquakes in 1840 and 1857.

The bells of the mission were recast and now ring out from the large church overlooking the small plaza. A piece of the original brick flooring is carefully preserved in the courtyard, but the tiny remaining portion of the burial ground in back of the church, surrounded by its crumbling adobe wall, is not quite so well maintained.

Across School Street from the mission is an adobe duplex probably built before the mission. It once served as guardhouse for Spanish soldiers accompanying the clergy.

At 109 Sylvar Street is a one-story house, believed to be the first wood frame dwelling in the community. Next door, a three-story Victorian stands behind an iron fence and manicured gardens—on the site of the city's first hotel and tavern. You will see numerous nineteenth-century houses on both sides of Mission Street.

Part of the town's first Protestant church forms

the nucleus of the house at 123 Green. On Highland Avenue, you can view a pink Victorian recently restored to its original beauty.

The beach parks

The coast in the Santa Cruz-Capitola area is dotted with excellent beach parks. Most of them have clean, wide beaches and are popular with swimmers and surf fishermen. The water is warmer here than along the coast farther north, and the surf is usually gentle.

Three miles west of Santa Cruz, Natural Bridges Beach State Park is an excellent surf fishing, swimming, and picnicking park, and its beautifully arched bridges are a favorite subject of painters and photographers. The two bridges (the sea is forming a third one), with arches about 35 feet high and spans of about 50 to 60 feet, were formed by the scouring action of waves, which pound incessantly against a finger-like peninsula of sandstone that juts out into the surf. The bridges are a prominent feature on the beach and can also be seen from the road along the top of the cliff.

Twin Lakes Beach State Park, within the Santa Cruz city limits, is a favorite with local residents. Camping is not permitted, but there are picnic facilities and firepits. One lagoon in the park is a wildfowl refuge; a second has been developed into a 350-berth small craft harbor.

Capitola Beach State Park is a small park operated by the city of Capitola. It is an amusement area with rides and a carnival atmosphere. There's a swimming beach, and the city also maintains a fresh-water pool at the mouth of Soquel Creek.

Campsites are available at New Brighton and Sunset state beaches. Seacliff State Beach offers trailer hookups and fishing from a unique pier—a 435-foot cement ship, *Palo Alto*. Zmudowski and Manresa state beach parks are day-use-only parks.

Begonia gardens

The Santa Cruz-Capitola area is an important growing center for tuberous begonias, and a visit to one of the large begonia nurseries is well worth while. August and September are the best months to see spectacular displays of the showy plants. (In Santa Cruz, Antonelli Brothers Begonia Gardens, 2545 Capitola Road, is open daily from 8:30 A.M. to 5:30 P.M. Admission is free, and group tours can be arranged by advance notice.) You can enjoy and photograph thousands of the colorful blooms as you stroll through the extensive lathhouses and greenhouses. You can buy plants in bloom, or you can place orders for tubers, to be delivered the following spring. In September, Capitola holds its Begonia Festival.

LATE SUMMER produces spectacular displays of color at begonia gardens in Santa Cruz-Capitola area.

Forest of Nisene Marks State Park

Most of the 9,750 acres of Nisene Marks State Park are still wild—with the coast hills covered with natural groves of oak, Douglas fir, madrone, bay, alder, maple, and redwood. The shiny ferns are untrampled, and there are no fences, litter cans, or marked walkways. Visitors can stroll along the dirt road sampling the terrain, breathing the clean air, enjoying the quiet.

To reach the park take the Aptos exit off State 1. Once in town, cross Aptos Creek and take the first street to the left, Aptos Creek Road (Eppler Drive), which heads into the park.

In the park the dirt road is very narrow, so drive cautiously. Three sections of the park, totaling 2,750 acres, are open to motor vehicles, but 1½ miles from the entrance you'll find the road closes; to explore the remaining 7,000 acres you must proceed on foot. Neither overnight camping nor fires are permitted in the park.

There are a number of redwood stumps 10 to 12 feet in diameter in the park, a result of heavy lumbering at the end of the 19th century. The lumbering left a few trees at the highest elevations, and some "mavericks," standing amid the logged area. These are the park's only virgin redwoods. The rest of the trees are about 60 years old.

MONTEREY PENINSULA AND ENVIRONS

Monterey • Carmel • San Simeon • Pinnacles

Cypress along 17-Mile Drive

The Monterey Peninsula, with its white sandy beaches, huge craggy rocks, pounding surf, and cypresses and pines, juts out into the Pacific Ocean south of Monterey Bay. Besides viewing one of the most picturesque spots on the Pacific shore, you can explore historic Monterey, browse through the shops of quaint Carmel, and drive through the densely wooded Del Monte Forest.

The peninsula's proximity to the ocean readily influences its weather. The summer months are apt to be overcast, with an early morning or late evening fog rolling in. In the fall, the days are warm and the sky crystal clear. Rain is frequent from December to March, but even in January, the wettest month, there will be crisp sunny days.

On the peninsula, there are numerous accommodations, from modern motels to old hotels. For a listing of places to stay, write to the Monterey Chamber of Commerce, 353 Camino el Estero, Monterey 93940.

State Highway 1, from north or south, takes you right through the Monterey Peninsula. If you want to follow the coastline, exit from the highway and follow the 17-Mile Drive (see page 83).

South of the peninsula, on State 1, the area is almost unpopulated. On your way to San Simeon, you will pass through Big Sur country, with the ocean on one side and the Santa Lucia Range on the other. Inland, U.S. Highway 101 will take you to Soledad, Pinnacles National Monument, and King City.

MONTEREY

Juan Rodriguez Cabrillo, a Portuguese explorer sailing for Spain, discovered Monterey Bay in 1542, and Sebastian Vizcaino visited the bay in 1602. However, it was not until 1770 that the area was settled. On the south shore of the bay, Gaspar de Portola and Father Junipero Serra established the first of Spain's four California presidios and the second of the Franciscans' 21 Alta California missions. One year later, Father Serra moved the mission to its present site on the Carmel River.

Until the middle of the 19th century, Monterey was California's liveliest and most important settlement. It began that century as the Spanish capital of Alta California; in 1822 it became the Mexican capital and in 1846 the American capital. After the discovery of gold in 1848, San Francisco took over as California's number one city. Monterey's 20th-century role centers around its fishing industry, and tourist and waterfront attractions.

You will find many echoes of the old Spanish and Mexican village of Monterey in today's modern town of 27,000. Many buildings constructed before 1850 still stand, most in good repair. Eleven of them are preserved as historical monuments by the state of California (see page 84). In downtown Monterey, you can follow the dashed red line which guides you past many of these old structures.

One of Monterey's historic buildings

Monterey's Municipal Pier and Marina

Along the waterfront

The Municipal Wharf extends out into Monterey Bay from the foot of Figueroa Street. Here you can watch commercial fishing boats unload anchovy, cod, kingfish, herring, salmon, sole, and tuna. Seven fish-processing plants share space at the end of this wharf. If you do not mind getting your feet damp, you can watch from doorways as workers clean and pack fish. Municipal Wharf is the best place for pier fishing (the catch ranges from sunfish to tomcod) and for viewing Monterey and its crescent-shaped bay.

Fisherman's Wharf, around the Monterey Marina four blocks west of Municipal Wharf, has novelty shops, a commercial aquarium, an art gallery, excursion boats, several restaurants, and a broad expansive plaza reminiscent of old Monterey. Sport fishing boats leave from here early every morning.

A seven-block stretch along Monterey Bay west of Fisherman's Wharf is Cannery Row, immortalized by John Steinbeck in his famous novel of the same name. Here in the early 1940's record sardine catches supported 16 canneries. By 1947 the sardines had almost completely disappeared, causing just about all the canneries to close down. Today as you enter Cannery Row, you drive under the covered conveyor belts which once carried the canned fish from the canneries to the warehouse. Many of the old buildings have been renovated, and you can browse through an art gallery and an antique shop, eat at one of several restaurants, or watch a film at the Steinbeck Theater. There are still some reminders of Steinbeck's novel—at 800 Cannery Row are the weathered clapboards of Doc Ricketts' Western Biological Laboratory; across the street is Wing Chong's, the "Lee Chong's Grocery" of the book; and down the block is the Bear Flag Inn.

Presidio of Monterey

Founded in 1770 by Gaspar de Portola, the Monterey Presidio is a sub post for the 22,000-acre Fort Ord Area; the site of the Defense Language Institute, West Coast Branch (where 24 foreign languages are taught); and the Training Center Human Research Unit.

The main gate is at Pacific and Artillery streets, near the site where Sebastian Vizcaino landed in 1602 and Father Junipero Serra and Captain Portola founded Monterey in 1770. A drive up the Corporal Ewing Road to the motor pool will take you to a life-sized statue of Father Serra. West of the Father Serra monument is a memorial to Commodore John Sloat, who in 1846 declared Monterey a possession of the United States. Stone from every county in California was used to make this memorial. A bust of Sloat is carved in the stone pedestal of the monument; an eagle overlooks the bay.

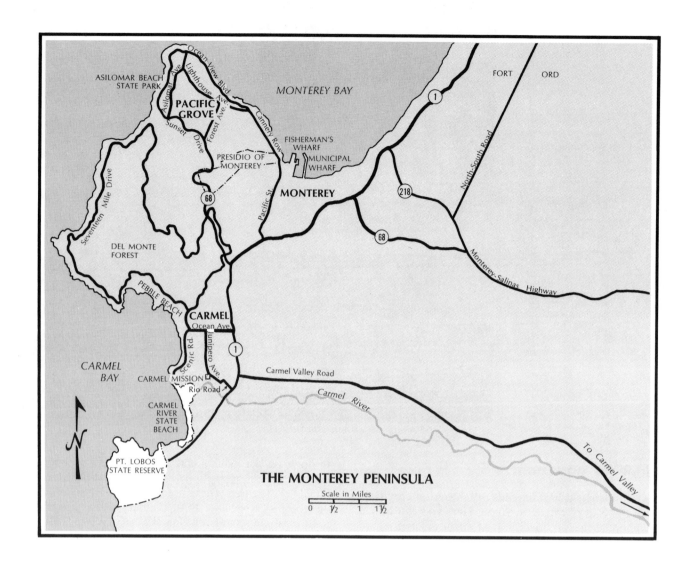

THE MONTEREY PENINSULA

Scale in Miles

0   ½   1   1½

Naval Postgraduate School

Just east of downtown Monterey, alongside State Highway 1, are the grounds of the old Del Monte Hotel, once one of the most elegant resorts in California. In 1947 the hotel was purchased by the U.S. Navy and turned into the Naval Postgraduate School in 1951.

Visitors are welcome to stroll through the campus daily between 9 A.M. and 4 P.M. The grounds contain more than 1,200 exotic trees, Del Monte Lake, and landscaped gardens. The hotel buildings remain, although they have been converted into classrooms and offices. Herrmann Hall boasts hand-painted ceilings, wrought-iron chandeliers, a now-unused fountain that extends along one wall from floor to ceiling.

To reach the school, turn onto Aguajito Road from State 1; then turn right on 3rd Street to the main entrance.

PACIFIC GROVE

The Methodists founded Pacific Grove in 1875 when they held the first of many seashore camp meetings here. The town was incorporated in 1889 with ordinances strictly regulating dancing, drinking, and public bathing. Today's Pacific Grove is more relaxed.

The Monarch butterfly (*Anosia plexippus*) is the Pacific Grove symbol. Starting in October thousands of Monarchs fly in to winter in a 6-acre grove of "Butterfly Trees" (follow the signs at the end of Lighthouse Avenue). Their fall arrival is celebrated with a big annual parade.

Just north of the intersection of Lighthouse and Asilomar avenues is the Point Pinos Lighthouse, which has stood at the entrance to Monterey Harbor since 1855. On the first floor of the lighthouse is a Coast Guard historical museum open to the public from 1 to 4 P.M. Saturday and Sunday. Surrounding the light station is a Coast Guard reservation where deer roam protected and fishermen fish from the rocky shoreline. The original lighthouse of granite and mortar was rebuilt of reinforced concrete after the 1906 earthquake. Automation is planned for the future, so the two-man crew will no longer have to check hourly on the light, radio, and foghorn.

At Forest and Central avenues is the Natural History Museum, where animal, vegetable, and mineral life of the Monterey Peninsula are on display. Of particular interest is the relief map of the peninsula and bay. You can see the great chasm of Monterey Bay, which goes down 8,400 feet, deeper than the Grand Canyon. The museum is open daily from 10 A.M. to 5 P.M.

At Municipal Beach along Ocean View Boulevard is Lovers Point. Here is a protected beach, a heated salt-water pool, and a good place to picnic. A short distance east of the beach is Point Cabrillo where Stanford University maintains the Hopkins Marine Laboratories. Ideal weather and water conditions make possible extensive research in hydrobiology. The laboratories are not open to the public.

Fronting the ocean side of the Monterey Peninsula is Asilomar Beach State Park, often used for large group conferences. If you cannot find hotel space on the peninsula, rustic and comfortable rooms are sometimes available at Asilomar.

17-MILE DRIVE

The 17-Mile Drive, wholly contained within the 4,280-acre Del Monte Forest, is an exceptionally scenic route. For 17 miles you drive through thickly wooded areas, see spectacular views of Monterey Bay, and swing along the breathtaking rocky coastal shore. At each of the four entrance gates (fee is $3 per car) you will receive a map of the route with points of interest clearly shown. It is easy to drive this 17-mile route—just follow the yellow line.

Along the drive you will see weathered Monterey cypresses, whose branches and foliage have been dramatically distorted by the sea winds. At Seal and Bird Rocks are black cormorants, sea ducks, sea gulls, and Leopard or Harbor Seals. Between the shore and the rocks are the sea lions.

Overnight camping is not allowed within the Del Monte Forest; however, you can picnic in specified areas. Fishing is permitted from Fanshell Beach north; hunting is not allowed. Within the Forest there are more than 100 miles of bridle trails.

Along the south shore of the peninsula on Carmel Bay is Pebble Beach. Here are the famous Pebble Beach Golf Course (one of six within the forest), the Del Monte Lodge (resort hotel), and exclusive homes.

LOOKING EAST from Fisherman's Wharf, you see pleasure boats anchored at Monterey's smallcraft harbor.

PACIFIC GROVE'S shoreline shows spectacular meeting of rock and wave; has a variety of underwater sea life.

A TOUR OF HISTORIC MONTEREY

Many Spanish-style adobes were constructed during the early 1800's to accommodate the 2,000 residents of Monterey. When New England seamen arrived, they modified the Spanish colonial design and created the "Monterey style"—two-storied adobes with a balcony. Many of the old buildings have disappeared; however, eleven buildings have been preserved and are maintained as the Monterey State Historical Monument.

These historical structures are close to the downtown area and the harbor. A good place to start is at the Custom House near Fisherman's Wharf.

• The Custom House, at 1 Custom Plaza, is the oldest government building on the Pacific Coast. Here the United States Flag was officially raised for the first time by Commodore John Sloat in 1846. This building was the collection center for revenue from foreign shipping until 1867, when it was abandoned. Today, the interior has been restored to appear as it originally did. The Custom House is open daily from 10 a.m. to 5 p.m.

• The Pacific House, at 8 Custom House Plaza, dates back to 1847. This building was first used by the U.S. Quartermaster for military offices and storage and later housed a tavern. Now a museum, the first floor contains exhibits of California history and the second floor a collection of American Indian artifacts. You can visit this landmark daily from 10 a.m. to 5 p.m.

• Casa del Oro is so named because of the unverified story that the building was once used as a gold depository. A general merchandise store in the 1850's, Casa del Oro stands at the corner of Scott and Oliver streets and displays trade items from early Monterey days. It is open daily from 10 a.m. to 5 p.m.

• Built in 1846-47, California's First Theater, at the corner of Scott and Pacific streets, is open daily except Tuesday from 10 a.m. to 5 p.m. Once a week a theater group presents 19th-century plays. The old bench seats still remain, and walls of the barroom are lined with old theatrical mementoes.

• Casa Soberanes, at 336 Pacific, is a private residence and is not open to the public. However, it is an excellent example of "Monterey-style" architecture.

• The Colton Hall, on Pacific Street, was built in 1847-49 and is the largest and most impressive of the old buildings. A museum on the second floor displays early government documents.

• The Larkin House, which dates back to 1835, is an excellent example of "Monterey-style" architecture. The two-storied adobe surrounded on three sides by a balcony was built by Thomas Larkin, U.S. Consul. A few of the furnishings are original pieces. This home, at the corner of Jefferson Street and Calle Principal, is open to the public Wednesday through Monday. Visitors are taken on a 35-minute guided tour—the first tour leaves at 10 a.m. and the last at 4 p.m.

• At Calle Principal near Madison is Casa Gutierrez, a typical adobe home of the Mexican Period. It is operated as a Mexican restaurant.

• The Stevenson House, named for Robert Louis Stevenson, who lived in this building during his short sojourn in Monterey in 1879, dates back to the late 1830's. At 530 Houston Street, the restored building devotes several rooms to Stevenson's personal mementoes. The house is open daily from 10 a.m. to 5 p.m.

• The Royal Presidio Chapel of San Carlos de Borromeo was founded in 1770 by Father Junipero Serra. The original hastily-constructed mud structure was rebuilt with a baroque facade by Father Serra's successor in 1794. A simple wooden cross is atop the chapel. Inside, several statues and Stations of the Cross are contemporary with the founding of the chapel. The chapel, on Church Street, is still in use today; visitors are welcome daily from 7 a.m. to 8 p.m.

• The U.S. Army Museum, in the Presidio of Monterey, (see map page 82) exhibits military items from early Spanish days to the present. The museum is open Wednesday through Friday from 10 a.m. to 5 p.m., Saturday and Sunday from 11 a.m. to 5 p.m.

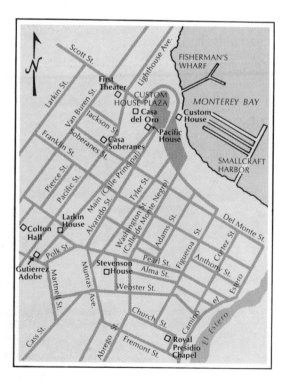

CARMEL

Since its first settlement, Carmel has tried to remain a simple village by the ocean. Even today houses have no street numbers, and there is no mail delivery (everyone goes to the post office). Downtown there are no billboards, no large retail signs, and at night no flood lighting and almost no street lighting. On the side streets you see no curbs, no sidewalks. A street sign may perch capriciously 10 feet in the air, or it may be missing entirely.

This is a village of shops—more than 150 of them, mostly small. And the shopping is good. Specialties are casual clothing for both men and women, often from Scotland, England, or Italy; art and craft work of all kinds, much of it produced locally; decorative imports from Mexico, Sweden, France, Italy; basketry, pottery, furniture from Japan and Hong Kong. Shopping is a tourist pastime in Carmel. The sidewalks are crowded on weekends, and the main street is jammed with cars.

Carmel is a village in a forest, and the forest is encouraged. The village forestry commission, busy with reforestation, has planted new street trees (mostly Monterey pines) between older trees.

Carmel has always respected its artists, writers, and craftsmen. Many serious artists who live here display their works in several downtown galleries. The Carmel Art Association maintains a sales gallery on Dolores Street.

One of the yearly attractions here is the Bach Festival, a week-long program of concerts held each July.

Carmel has several hotels and a large number of motels, inns, and guest cottages; yet advance room reservations are advisable in summer, and especially during such events as the Bach Festival.

In exploring Carmel, you will see a variety of architecture. The early rough summer cabins have given way to Hansel and Gretel-type structures and Monterey-style adobe homes. Fronting the ocean are some very modern homes, including a Frank Lloyd Wright design. One of Carmel's most widely known residences is Tar House, home of poet Robinson Jeffers until his death in 1962. The house is at Scenic Road and Stewarts Way and is distinguished by a large stone tower which Jeffers himself built.

Carmel beach

Carmel's beautiful beach is for walkers and, in good weather, sunbathers. The beach is unsafe for swimming, but most bathers find the water too cold anyway. Along Scenic Road, which runs along the water, you will see dark gnarled cypresses, sparkling white sand, and crashing surf. At the southern end of the beach, the shoreline becomes rocky and has many tidepools.

OCEAN AVENUE, Carmel's main street, is lined with small shops that invite those who love to browse.

CARMEL MISSION, dedicated in 1797, is distinguished by star window, unequal towers, rough sandstone walls.

South of the village limits at the end of Scenic Drive the beach becomes Carmel River State Beach. Here you can picnic around a beach fire or splash in the lagoon of Carmel River.

Carmel Mission

South of the town proper just off State 1 at Rio Road (or follow Junipero Avenue south) is Mission San Carlos Borromeo del Rio Carmelo. Fully restored through the efforts of craftsmen, benefactors, and clergy, the mission provides one of the most authentic and picturesque links with early California history. The mission is open to visitors Monday through Friday from 9 A.M to 5 P.M., Sunday from 1 to 5 P.M.

In the mission museum are the original silver altar pieces brought by Father Junipero Serra from Baja California and the restored refectory of Father Serra. Behind the mission is a cemetery where 3,000 Indians are buried.

POINT LOBOS STATE RESERVE

Just south of Carmel on State 1, the 1,250-acre Point Lobos State Reserve is one of the most beautiful spots on the California coast. Here you can hike, picnic, explore tide pools, sun on the beach, or fish.

The best way to explore Point Lobos is to hike over some of its well kept trails. The Seal Rocks trail takes you through yellow and white-flowered sagebrush to an expanse of rock that pushes into the ocean. From here you can watch sea lions and seals sunning themselves on the offshore rocks. Because of the barking of these sea animals, the Spanish called this area *Puna de los Lobos Marinos* or Point of the Sea Wolves.

Perhaps the most scenic trail is the one that takes you along the north side of the Point Lobos cliffs, a piece of the point which is inaccessible by automobile. The trail, lined with pines, starts at Whaler's Cove, climbs up to Cannery Point, and skirts around Bluefish Cove. From this height—about 50 feet above the water—you look down to the pounding surf of the green-blue ocean. (Although the trail is safe, it is not recommended for young children.)

The south shore trail passes several pebbly beaches and branches off to two sandy beaches. China Beach is small and secluded, while Gibson Beach is broad and less protected.

Around the headland and shoreline, low tides expose rocky pools teeming with marine creatures. Colonies of sea urchins, sea anemones, starfish, and scuttling hermit crabs are a few of the more conspicuous inhabitants. On prominent rocks you will see sea gulls and on Bird Island cormorants and brown pelicans.

If you visit Point Lobos in November, you might see the California gray whale which travels close to shore here on its annual 12,000-mile migration to Lower California. Between 1861 and 1884 Whaler's Cove was used as a whaling station. From the trail between park headquarters and the cove you will see a remnant from these days—a whaler's weathered cottage.

Point Lobos is open daily from 9 A.M. to 5 P.M. (to 7 P.M. in the summer). The entrance fee is 75 cents per car. There are sites for picnicking, but camping and fires are not permitted.

CARMEL VALLEY

South of Carmel, the Carmel Valley Road turns east from State 1 and heads inland along the Carmel River. As you drive through the valley, you will pass artichoke fields, fruit orchards, strawberry patches, and cattle grazing the slopes of the rolling hills.

Carmel Valley is a vacationland. Its weather is warm and clear—ideal for such outdoor sports as fishing, hunting, horseback riding, and swimming. Near the mouth of the Carmel Valley, spanning both sides of the Carmel River, are two new championship golf courses—available for public play. The Carmel River holds an abundance of trout, and during the annual spawning season steelhead salmon are plentiful. In the nearby Santa Lucia Mountains you can hunt wild boar and deer. For a list of accommodations and facilities available, write to the Carmel Valley Chamber of Commerce, Box 217, Carmel Valley.

If you are in the Carmel Valley, you might want to visit the Bavarian Mushroom Farm. Turn north off Carmel Valley Road about one mile after entering the valley. Five miles farther east are begonia gardens where 15,000 begonias are a massive wheel of color in the summer.

SOUTH ALONG THE COAST

From Carmel, as you drive south on State 1, you cross Bixby Creek Bridge, 260 feet above the creek bed. You can park your car at the far end of the bridge and walk back on the catwalk to some observation alcoves for a view of the surf, beach, and headlands. The road south then dips and rises as it follows the rugged coastline.

You will pass Point Sur Lighthouse perched on a headland of rock. The lighthouse is open to visitors Monday through Friday from 1 to 3 P.M., Saturday, Sunday, and holidays from 1 to 4 P.M. A warning is flashed from the lighthouse every 15 seconds and can be seen for 25 miles out to sea.

South of Point Sur the highway swings inland through stands of redwoods along the Big Sur River to Pfeiffer Big Sur State Park. The campgrounds are apt to be crowded, so reservations are advisable, especially in the summer or on weekends. Here you can picnic, hike (some trails lead out to Los Padres National Forest), swim, or fish upstream in the river. Hotel-type accommodations and housekeeping cabins are available at Big Sur Lodge.

Three miles south of Pfeiffer Big Sur State Park is Nepenthe. The redwood pavilion, designed by a student of Frank Lloyd Wright's, sits 800 feet above the sea and affords a superb view of southern Big Sur. Nepenthe opens every day at 12 noon. Besides housing a restaurant, it has become an informal social-cultural center for the Big Sur region.

South of Nepenthe, just beyond Partington Point, a steep, narrow road leaves State 1 and climbs up to the homes occupied by the Partington Ridge colony of Big Sur artists, writers, and craftsmen.

Below Kirk Creek Bridge, a precipitous road leaves State 1 at Mill Creek, loops into the mountains, climbs to 3,200 feet at Nacimiento Summit, and drops down to 1,200 feet along the Nacimiento River. You can continue on the road up to Mission San

CARMEL VALLEY'S rolling hills, warm climate, country atmosphere attract retired people, resort enthusiasts.

Antonio de Padua (see page 89) and to King City and U.S. 101.

State 1, south of the Mill Creek turnoff, becomes somewhat rough and winding in places. Around Pacific Valley, you will find rough trails that go down the cliffs to Jade Beach. In this well-scoured area— a mile or more of rocky beaches—your best chances of finding small bits of jadeite or nephrite are during low tides.

Four bridges and 12 miles farther is Salmon Creek Bridge, marking the southern boundary of the Monterey District of Los Padres National Forest. This is also just about the southern limit of the coast redwoods (*Sequoia sempervirens*) and the Douglas fir (*Pseudotsuga macrocarpa*). At Salmon Creek a pleasant trail follows the stream into a canyon. It is fairly level for about a mile, then is a rather stiff climb for the next 2 miles. At the mouth of the canyon is a waterfall that drops over the rocks at the ocean's edge.

SANTA LUCIA RANGE provides scenic backdrop to San Simeon (Hearst Castle). Twin ivory-colored towers belong to main mansion.

NATIONAL MONUMENT preserves pinnacles created by volcano.

San Simeon

The Hearst San Simeon State Historical Monument, a collection of mansions, terraced gardens, pools, sculpture, and exotic trees, occupies 123 acres atop a spur of the Santa Lucia Mountains. The focal point is *La Casa Grande*, a 137-foot-high structure which resembles a Spanish cathedral. However, its imposing ridge-top position has given it the aspect of a castle when viewed from afar.

In 1922 construction began on *La Casa Grande*, William Randolph Hearst's private residence. Hearst never referred to his home as a castle, but called the estate *La Cuesta Encantada*—The Enchanted Hill. Money was no object—Hearst imported furniture, antiques, Gothic and Renaissance tapestries, fine wood carvings, French and Italian fire mantels, carved ceilings, silver, Persian rugs, and Roman mosaics.

Hearst also imported wildlife, and today zebras, tahr goats, and Barbary sheep still roam on the grounds. To landscape the grounds, topsoil replaced the barren soil of the hilltop, and special plants, trees, and vines were planted among the native oaks.

San Simeon is located on State 1, about 94 miles south of Monterey. Three separate tours, each about 2 hours long, are conducted through the estate. Tour 1 includes the gardens, the Neptune and Roman pools, the ground floor of La Casa Grande (assembly hall, refectory, billiard room, theater, kitchen, and service areas), and one of the three guest houses. Tour 2 covers the upper levels of the mansion (main library, cloister bedrooms, Hearst's personal suite, and Celestial Suite). Self-guiding tour 3 takes you through the North Guest Wing. Reservations for the tours can be obtained by writing to the Department of Parks and Recreation, P.O. Box 2390, Sacramento 95811. Tour prices are $3 for tours 1 and 3, $4 for tour 2, half price for children. Each tour begins at the foot of Enchanted Hill; you park your car in the parking lot and board a bus for the ride up the hill.

INLAND SIDE TRIPS

Two inland routes parallel the coastal highway and offer sights well worth seeing. U.S. 101 heads south through the valley of the Salinas River, while State Highway 25 crosses the San Benito River in the coastal range.

Pinnacles National Monument

At Pinnacles National Monument spires and crags, remains of a volcanic mountain, rise up to 1,200 feet above the canyon floors and present a sharp contrast to the surrounding smooth countryside.

The best way to appreciate fully the extraordinary features here is to hike on some of the trails. On the east side short and easy trips are in the cave area around Bear Gulch, where the visitor center and picnic area are located. The High Peaks Trail is more strenuous.

There are campgrounds at Chalone Creek and Chaparral. A group reservation camp is at Chalone Annex. On the Soledad side of the monument, you walk into the narrow defile between the overhangs of Machete Ridge and The Balconies. Huge boulders close the caves to natural light (be sure to carry a flashlight). You will have to crawl, stretch, duck, and squeeze along for a few hundred feet until you come to daylight and the other end of the cave. Children should not go in the caves alone; with a light there is little danger in the caves, but in the dark slippery places, low ceilings and drop-offs are hazardous.

Pinnacles National Monument is just off State 25, 35 miles south of Hollister. You can also reach the Pinnacles via U.S. 101 by turning onto State Highway 146 at Soledad. However, this road does not go all the way through the monument, and you will be unable to reach the visitor center. Fall through spring are the best months to visit the monument; the summer months are quite hot.

Soledad Mission ruins

A turn westward off U.S. 101 just south of Soledad will take you past a frame and adobe building on your right. This is Los Coches, former headquarters of a large ranch, part of the lands of Mission Nuestra Senora de la Soledad (Our Lady of Solitude).

A drive of half a mile west of Los Coches and a turn to the north will take you to the wind-swept beet fields on which are several crumbling walls, all that remain of the original mission. A modern chapel was erected here by the Native Daughters of the Golden West.

From the mission ruins, you can backtrack to U.S. 101 or take the back roads to Carmel and Monterey.

Drive south up the steep Arroyo Seco Road, following its turn in a westerly direction to Paloma Creek Road. This is a dirt road, which is unsatisfactory within 24 hours after rain. After 18 miles of winding through rangeland dotted with oaks, eucalyptus, sycamores, and pines, you will be back on the paved Carmel Valley Road.

Mission San Antonio de Padua

One of the most completely restored of all California missions, Mission San Antonio de Padua still remains somewhat isolated. To reach it, exit off U.S. 101 at King City and follow the road for 18 miles to Jolon. Visitors are welcome Monday through Friday from 9 A.M. to 4:30 P.M., Sunday from 11 A.M. to 5 P.M.

Mission San Antonio de Padua is reminiscent of the missions as they were during the days of the padres. In place of the crumbling adobe walls are buildings considered to be replicas of those that existed in the prosperous years between 1771 and 1830. Some of the original tiles are on the roof.

Besides the mission itself, there is a water-powered grist mill, a tannery, the original wine vat, and exhibits of early mission art and replicas of mission equipment.

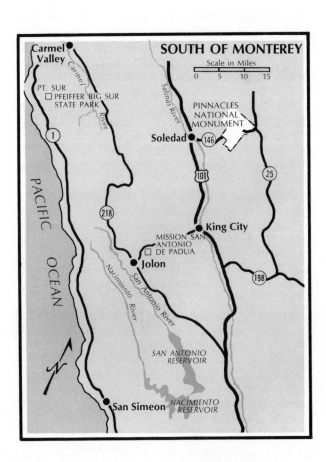

THE CENTRAL VALLEY

Sacramento • The Delta • Valley Parks
San Joaquin and Sacramento Rivers

State capitol at Sacramento

The flat Central Valley provides a strong contrast to the surrounding mountainous land—on the east are the Sierra Nevada Mountains and on the west the Coast Range. To the south rise the Tehachapis, and to the north the foothills of the southern Cascades and the northern Coast Range meet.

The Central Valley extends 465 road miles from north to south and is 30 to 60 miles wide. The Valley actually includes two valleys—the Sacramento through which the Sacramento River flows, and the San Joaquin named for the river that runs part way through it.

Agriculture is the mainstay of the Central Valley. The area is supported by fruit orchards, vineyards, and staple crops such as onions, sweet potatoes, and grain. These lands are grazing grounds for dairy cattle and livestock. Two inland ports—at Sacramento and Stockton—have opened up the landlocked valley and have given these products easy access to the sea.

The most traveled route between Southern and Northern California— State Highway 99—runs right through the Central Valley. When completed, Interstate Highway 5 on the valley's western side will be an alternate route.

Although the Central Valley extends south below Bakersfield, the section identified with Northern California ends at Fresno. For a description of the southern part of the Valley, see the *Sunset Travel Guide to Southern California.*

SACRAMENTO

Most of the major highway routes through Western California pass through Sacramento, the state capital. To the east, Interstate 80 and U.S. Highway 50 lead into the Sierra, to Lake Tahoe, and into Nevada. For southern travel, State 99 is the main artery. To the north, State 99 and Interstate 5, which unite at Red Bluff, lead into the northern mountains. The main route to the San Francisco Bay Area is Interstate 80.

A deep water channel to San Francisco Bay has made Sacramento a seaport. Deep-sea ships travel 90 miles inland to serve the landlocked counties to the north and east. The Port of Sacramento is a major loading facility for the rich agricultural products of the Valley.

Capital of the state since 1854, Sacramento still has many charming old residential areas. Downtown, most of the old houses have gradually given way to modern office buildings and apartments, but if you drive some of the wide, tree-shaded side streets, you can see handsome old homes fronted by cool-looking green lawns and colorful gardens.

The State Capitol

Dominating the city is the domed capitol building, surrounded by Capitol Park with its well groomed

Sacramento River near Colusa

Fishermen and freighter sharing The Delta

lawns and flower beds. The park, an oasis on warm Valley days, has 40 acres of more than 40,000 trees, shrubs, and plants. You can see plants and trees from all over the world, including a collection of trees brought from Civil War battlefields. Of camellias alone, there are more than 800 varieties among some 2,200 plantings. Best time to see them in bloom is in February and March.

The capitol building, completed in 1874, is open from 7 A.M. to 9 P.M. Tours are given daily at 1 and 2:30 P.M. with 10 and 11 A.M. tours added Monday through Friday. On weekday afternoons while the legislature is in session (February and March in even-numbered years, January to June in odd-numbered years), you can watch the Senate or Assembly from the visitors' galleries. If a bill is up for an assembly vote, you can see each vote registered—the assemblyman pushes a button on his desk which flashes red for "no" and green for "yes" on a board.

The State Library

The State Library (open Monday through Friday from 8 A.M. to 5 P.M.) is housed in a handsome granite building adjoining the capitol building. The general reading room is adorned with a Maynard Dixon mural depicting California history. An excellent file of present and past California newspapers is maintained for your perusal.

E. B. Crocker Art Gallery

The Crocker Art Gallery, 216 O Street, was built by Edwin B. Crocker in 1873 to house his private collection. The stately building with its Victorian interior —sweeping staircases, parquetry floors, repousse ceilings, and grand ballroom—houses a collection of European paintings, drawings, decorative arts, sculpture, and crafts. Of particular interest is its Oriental collection and its collection of contemporary American art.

A new wing has been recently added to the gallery and increases exhibition space by nearly half.

The gallery is open to the public Tuesday through Sunday from 10 A.M to 5 P.M.

Sutter's Fort

The town of Sacramento sprang up around Sutter's Fort after James Marshall discovered gold at nearby Coloma in 1848 (see page 104). Now the fort stands in the center of the city, housing a collection of gold rush artifacts, historical mementoes, and the State Indian Museum.

John Sutter built the fort in 1839 to protect his surrounding Mexican land grant of some 76 square miles. Here in 1844 he entertained the United States exploring party led by John C. Fremont and his

PARKWAY along Sacramento's American River has bicycle, hiking, bridle trails; boating and picnicking.

guide, Kit Carson, and during the Bear Flag Revolt of 1846, General Vallejo was detained here.

After the discovery of gold, Sutter lost his land to newcomers and later went East. In 1891-93 the state of California restored the fort following sketches and plans from Sutter's day.

To reach the fort, follow 16th Street in Sacramento to L Street and turn east. The fort is between 26th and 28th streets. It is open daily from 10 A.M. to 5 P.M. with no admission charge.

Old Sacramento

Imaginative individuals are restoring a 28-acre section of Sacramento's waterfront to recreate the colorful atmosphere of Sacramento in the 1850's and 1860's. Historical buildings are being restored and reconstructed on their original sites. Other structures of historical significance that were demolished for Interstate Highway 5 are being reconstructed in this new location.

Old Sacramento is on the eastern bank of the Sacramento River between Capitol Mall and the I Street Bridge viaduct, west of Interstate 5.

Horse-drawn street cars, wagons, carriages, and stagecoaches, wooden signs and painted awnings, and wooden plank sidewalks are intended to give Old Sacramento the look of its golden age. Five museums will tell the story of transportation and communication in the early West. The city-county museum will trace the physical development of the area from pre-Spanish days to the present.

Nine acres of Old Sacramento have been designated as a state historic park. Two special attractions will be the Big Four Building (one-time headquarters for the Central Pacific Railroad, financed by Huntington, Hopkins, Crocker and Stanford) and the railway display. The Big Four Building was carefully dismantled and is being reconstructed at I Street between Front and 2nd streets using the same bricks, artifacts, and hardware that composed the original. On the first floor a museum will show the original Huntington and Hopkins mercantile store and the Stanford store.

Among railway equipment to be displayed are the wood-burning Governor Stanford Engine #1, on loan to the state from Stanford University, and the Gold Coast, the luxurious private car of Lucius Beebe.

Chinese and Mexican trade centers

A new "Chinatown" is being developed around the Confucius Temple at 4th and I streets. Buildings of Oriental design are being constructed, and a landscaped pedestrian mall will feature a Chinese garden. Chinatown will include residences, commercial stores, offices, and restaurants.

A Mexican Cultural and Trade Center will occupy the block bounded by 5th, 6th, I, and J streets. Three Spanish-style buildings will contain small retail shops and offices, while a fourth building will be a cultural and community center. A central plaza will host concerts and folk dancing.

William Land Park

This park on Freeport Boulevard (State Highway 160 and Sutterville Road) in the southern part of the city is so vast it seldom seems crowded. There is a midway with ponies, small trains, and a merry-go-round; duck ponds; Fairytale Town; a 9-hole golf course; baseball fields; and a large zoo.

Gibson Ranch County Park

Just north of downtown Sacramento is 245-acre Gibson Ranch County Park. To reach the park, follow Watt Avenue north to Elverta Road. Turn left onto Elverta and follow this road a short distance to the park. Gibson Ranch is open daily from 7 A.M. to dusk.

Children will enjoy seeing domestic animals, peacocks, and pheasants and watching milking demonstrations which are regularly scheduled. An 8-acre lake is stocked with fish (children under 16 do not need a fishing license) and is a natural habitat for ducks, mudhens, geese, and muskrats.

One of the ranch buildings houses an historical museum displaying western objects. There is a blacksmith shop where you can watch horses being shod. Stables rent horses and ponies, offer hayrides and riding lessons. The park has hiking trails and picnicking facilities.

American River Parkway

An irregular, 23-mile-long strip of green stretches along the banks of the American River from Nimbus Dam to the stream's junction with the Sacramento River. Along the American River Parkway are several county parks. C. M. Goethe County Park offers hiking and riding trails, Discovery Park has boat launching facilities, and Ancil Hoffman County Park an 18-hole golf course. The parkway has picnicking sites.

Fishing the American River produces catches of shad, steelhead, or salmon. Group float trips are popular on the river, with kayaks or rubber rafts the modes of transportation.

NORTH OF SACRAMENTO

The Sacramento Valley sprang up during the Gold Rush days when river steamers and sailing schooners on the Sacramento and Feather rivers opened up such communities as Marysville and Red Bluff to Sacramento. After gold panned out, agriculture developed, and irrigation enabled groves of figs, citrus, olives, and other fruits to be planted. Grain ranches were built close to the Sacramento River, and grain soon became the Valley's chief product.

The large grain fields were subsequently subdivided, and the smaller irrigated ranches were planted with orchards, citrus groves, vineyards, alfalfa, vegetable crops, and some newcomers—cotton, rice, and sugar beets. These crops have remained at the heart of the Valley's agriculture.

The major highways running north of Sacramento are Interstate 5 and State 99. Both leave from Sacramento with Interstate 5 taking a more westerly course. In Red Bluff both highways converge and Interstate 5 continues into Oregon. The Sacramento River runs between both highways, while the Feather closely parallels State 99.

The Sacramento River

Upstream from Sacramento as far as Colusa, the Sacramento is a river of commerce, although the commercial traffic it bears today (mostly tugs and oil barges) is insignificant compared to that of the past. Remnants of yesterday can be seen in places

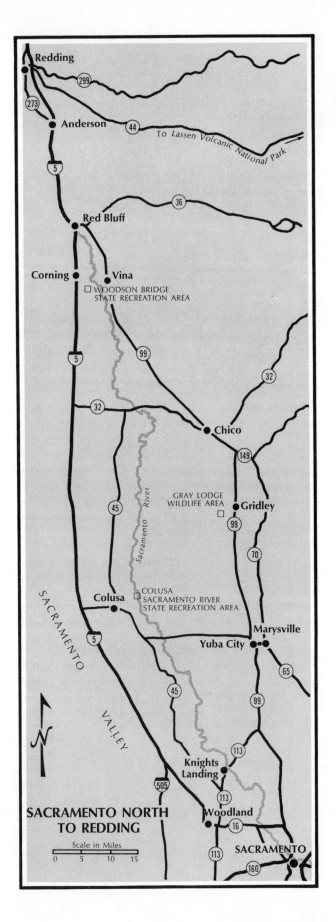

WILDFOWL preen and wade in shallow resting ponds at Gray Lodge Wildlife Area in the Sacramento Valley.

along the river—occasionally you'll see half rotting wharves through the cottonwoods and willows that mark the sites of forgotten towns. The tall piers where steamers were tied up have been replaced by long floats for pleasure boating and fishing.

All the way to Red Bluff, the Sacramento is a lowland river, but above Colusa it is almost wild. Interrupting the long, meandering, tree-walled stretches are occasional bars, riffles, and snags. Here kingfishers, herons, ducks, otter, and beaver make their home. Steelhead trout and king salmon push through the river in relentless migrations that overlap one another and make fishing an all-year sport.

Swimming and water skiing are possible almost anywhere along the Sacramento River, but the farther you are from Shasta Dam, the warmer the water will be. Colusa is the most popular water-skiing center, with public floats and a jumping ramp. The Colusa-Sacramento River State Recreation Area has a launching ramp, picnic sites, a sandy beach, and campsites.

Most of the towns and fishing resorts along the river have launching facilities for trailered boats. Motorless boats are suitable for downstream trips only. Rowing or paddling against the strong current is difficult, and at some points impossible. The water is not too rough for boats 14 feet or larger, even in the swiftest riffles. The biggest waves on the Sacramento are those made by passing barges and "speed-ers." But the current is something else—it may carry underpowered or stalled boats onto snags or rocks, or into the occasional overhanging branches.

Life jackets should always be worn while boating the upper Sacramento, and also while fishing along steep, slippery banks. Below Colusa, be careful not to tie up where barges might swing close to shore and strike your boat, or bounce it around in their wakes.

You can fish for salmon or steelhead in the waters of the Sacramento. The spring run of salmon begins in June, and the fall run, perhaps the most important, starts in late September and overlaps the steelhead migration that comes in October and November.

While most fishing is done from boats in the main current, bank fishing is perfectly practical. Cast far out, let your lure glide downstream, and then retrieve it against the current.

To fish from a boat, it is a good idea to hire a guide at one of the resorts for your first time out. He can show you where to find the best fishing spots, and how to handle your tackle there for the best results. If you take your own boat, be sure you have a good anchor to hold you against the current. Then the flow of the river will do your "trolling" for you.

There is only one cable ferry left on the Sacramento River and that is at Princeton, north of Colusa on State Highway 45. Here you and your car can be transported across the river on a ferry pulled from bank to bank by a cable.

Gray Lodge Wildlife Area

In late autumn and winter, ducks and geese from the Yukon, Saskatchewan, and British Columbia breeding grounds flock to the Central Valley. One of the best places to watch their massive migrations is at Gray Lodge Wildlife Area, just south of Gridley, 65 miles north of Sacramento via State 99.

Aquatic plants and cereal crops are grown on the 6,800-acre state reserve to entice wildfowl so they will not feast on surrounding private fields. One portion of the area is a wildlife sanctuary. On a larger section, hunting is permitted during the season. On hunting days you must obtain a pass before driving through the sanctuary.

At the area's headquarters is a small museum with more than a hundred specimens of birds that frequent the area. There is no entrance fee to the wildlife area, which is open daily during daylight hours.

Woodson Bridge State Recreation Area

Woodson Bridge State Recreation Area is on the Sacramento River, just 3 miles west of State Highway 99 at Vina or 6 miles east of Interstate 5 at Corning. The park is an almost unspoiled example of river bottom lands. Part of it is covered with oaks, while a flood plain section is densely wooded with willows, cottonwoods, and sycamores. The river bisects the park.

Park activities are swimming, boating, excellent fishing, hiking, and camping. The adjoining Tehama County Park has a small picnic area, a playground, and concessions.

Red Bluff's Victorians

The Victorian houses of Red Bluff stand grandly along tree-lined streets high above the banks of the Sacramento River. The colorful gold-seekers, trappers, Indians, and Chinese workers of the 19th century are long gone, and the city's historic hotel has been demolished, but many fine homes and stores of that eventful era remain.

You can visit the Kelly-Griggs House Museum built around 1880, at 311 Washington Street. Upstairs you'll see a furnished bedroom-sitting room suite and an old-fashioned bathroom. Three smaller rooms used for displays contain personal articles from pioneer days, Indian artifacts, and a collection of art spanning almost a century. Paintings on the stairway and in the halls depict Victorian scenes in the town.

At the Kelly-Griggs House Museum you can purchase the "windshield tour" map for 10 cents; it directs you past the Victorian homes in central Red Bluff.

The Ide Adobe

Along the west bank of the Sacramento River, near Red Bluff, the William B. Ide Adobe State Historical Monument is an oasis for travelers. You can picnic on verdant grounds overlooking the river or wander through the shady 4-acre park, once the home of the only president of California—when the state was a republic under the Bear Flag.

Original structures are the adobe ranch house (now a museum) and a hand-dug well. Since state acquisition of the site in 1951, the carriage house, smokehouse, and corral have been restored to suggest ranch life in the 1850's.

The monument is open daily from 8 A.M. to 5 P.M. with no admission charge. To reach the Adobe from Interstate 5, take State Highway 36 through Red Bluff. Turn right at Adobe Road; it is a mile to the entrance. Boaters will find mooring facilities near the site of the old Adobe Ferry.

Coleman National Fish Hatchery

The Coleman National Fish Hatchery, 11 miles southeast of Anderson on Ball's Ferry County Road, col-

lects 30 to 50 million chinook salmon eggs and two million steelhead eggs annually. Large numbers of salmon and steelhead are trapped at Keswick Dam and transported by tank trucks to the hatchery to be artificially spawned. The fish are reared for stocking the Sacramento River.

Visitors are welcome at the hatchery from 8 A.M. to 5 P.M. daily. Camping and picnicking sites are available.

Chico

Here is the most impressive—and unexpected—park in the whole Valley. It starts downtown with the campus of Chico State College and the colonial mansion of town founder John Bidwell. Then Bidwell Park winds up Chico Creek 10 miles into the foothills. There is swimming, golf, and picnicking. Its landmark is gigantic Hooker Oak, with a spread of 150 feet.

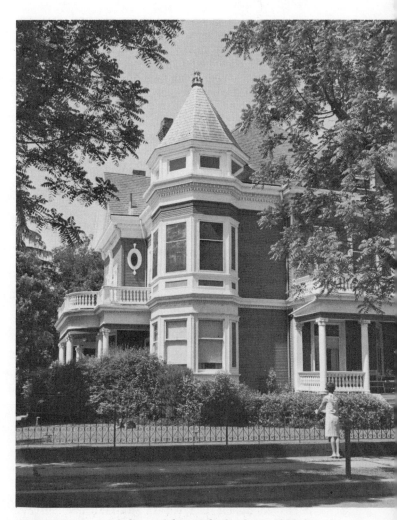

TURRETED and balconied home, built about 1900 in Queen Anne style, is on Red Bluff's tour of homes.

THE DELTA

The Sacramento-San Joaquin Delta is an irregularly bounded area of almost 740,000 acres. It extends from Sacramento south a little beyond Tracy, from Pittsburg east to Stockton. About 50,000 of its acres are water, strung out in more than 700 miles of meandering channels.

This area, once a great inland everglade, densely forested with stands of valley oak and bull pine, was devoured by the furnaces of the old river boats. The denuded expanses of mud that remained were later transformed into levee-rimmed islands (many are still called tracts) that produced fortunes in asparagus and fruits for Delta farmers.

The first "resorts" in this area were farmhouses that just happened to have a boat or two for rent. Reports of the excellent fishing began to spread, and small, makeshift fishing camps sprang up along the levee roads. Recreational fishing and boating became big business and resort marinas replaced the small fishing camps.

As you drive between Sacramento and Manteca on State 99, you're never more than 10 or 15 miles east of the Delta region, but you hardly know it is there. Until now, major highways have circumvented it entirely; however, Interstate 5, scheduled for completion in 1973, will cross the heart of the Delta.

Boating on the Delta

You do not have to be a boat owner to enjoy the cruising pleasure of the Delta. Here, there are more than a hundred marinas, resorts, harbors, and fishing camps which rent boats. Most of the rental fleet is 12 to 14-foot fishing skiffs and houseboats. The "floating motels" of the Delta range from small, non-powered barges ($8 to $10 a day) to luxurious, well appointed floating homes that sleep six or more and have electricity, running water, complete kitchens, and in some cases complete bathrooms. Rentals for one of these large, better-appointed houseboats run about $40 to $60 a day or $300 to $450 per week. Rates vary according to the number of persons aboard and the season.

The remainder of the Delta rental fleet is a mixed assortment of cruisers, ski boats, small sailboats, and miscellaneous small craft.

There is not much chance of getting seriously lost in the Delta, but it is easy to become temporarily confused about your exact whereabouts. A good map, marine chart, or guide book is essential for the newcomer. The basic guide to navigation in the Delta region is Harbor Chart No. 5527 (San Joaquin River) published by the U.S. Coast and Geodetic Survey. The chart costs $1 and is available from the Chart Distribution Division (C44), Washington D.C.

20235. The back of the San Joaquin chart contains a navigation guide to the Sacramento River from Andrus Island to Sacramento (Harbor Chart 5528) and includes the northern reaches of the Delta. The southern reaches of the Delta are covered on a small chart, 166-SC ($1.50). These charts indicate channel depths, bridge and overhead cable clearances, channel markers, and various hazards to navigation.

As the deep water channels of the Delta are also busy routes of marine commerce, pleasure boats should follow certain rules. For free pamphlets on California boating regulations and water safety, write to California Division of Small Craft Harbors, 1416 Ninth Street, Sacramento, or contact a district office of the U.S. Coast Guard.

Swimming and water-skiing

The waterways of the Delta are not the most inviting place for swimmers, but both swimming and water-skiing are popular despite the rather sluggish nature of the water. Considerate water-skiers avoid quiet anchorages in respect to fishermen.

Accommodations

Ideally, your boat will be your home on the waterways of the Delta. You'll find modern motels in the cities that lie along the edge of the Delta, and there is an occasional old charmer of a hotel in the river towns along the Sacramento, but adequate accommodations in the Delta proper are few and far between.

A few of the resort marinas offer housekeeping cabins or small campgrounds, and Brannan Island State Park (the only developed public campground in the Delta) has a 100-unit campground with facilities for trailers. Most of the larger resorts operate a snack bar, and there are a few isolated cafes, but for a full-scale dinner you will have to go to one of the larger towns on the outskirts. The seasoned Delta sailor brings almost all his own provisions.

Fishing

Fishing is an all-year activity in the Delta, but spring is a peak season for one of the Delta's most sought-after game fish—the striped bass. Salmon and steelhead pass through the Delta on their fall migration up the Sacramento River, but the Delta itself seldom presents the ideal water conditions for trout fishing.

Most of the resort operators in the Delta have been there a long time and can guide you to the best places for fishing. Probably the best source of up-to-date fishing information is *Weekend Outdoor News*, P.O. Box 1000, Woodland, California 95695. They also have a good map of the Delta.

HOUSEBOAT anchors in Delta slough, east of Sacramento River.

LOCKE'S two-story buildings rise only one story above levee. This Delta town is snug behind levee road about 30 miles south of Sacramento.

SOUTH OF SACRAMENTO

South of Sacramento the Central Valley follows the course of the San Joaquin River, which flows northward to meet the Sacramento River.

Agricultural development came later in this part of the Valley than in the Sacramento Valley. Stockton was a booming mining town in the 1850's, but south of here there was almost nothing. After the turn of the 20th century, the San Joaquin Valley began to grow, but it was the post-World War II boom that really developed the area.

State 99 and Interstate 5 (scheduled for completion in 1973) are the main routes south of Sacramento.

Lodi Lake

Big, tree-lined Lodi Lake on the north side of Lodi typifies water use in the Valley. Until the 1880's the lake site was swamp overflow from the Mokelumne River. An irrigation district dammed one end of the low place to catch high water from the river. The lake was at first privately owned but was given to the city of Lodi in 1934. Now it is a recreation spot offering boating, swimming, and picnicking.

Micke's Grove

Five miles south of Lodi and a mile west of State 99 by way of Armstrong Road, this 59-acre grove was the gift of the late William C. Micke, Lodi vineyardest. Now a San Joaquin County park, it contains one of the few remaining large stands of native valley oaks. Here you'll see a small garden zoo where flowers bloom all year under the oak trees and in planters that serve the unusual purpose of separating animals' cages. The park has no camping facilities.

The wineries

The Lodi and Fresno areas are famed for their sweet appetizer and dessert wines. Long, warm summers bring grapes to maximum sugar content. Some dozen wineries are open to visitors in the Lodi area, also the home of the Tokay grape (a table variety). Fresno is the hub of the other big wine district, and the majority of wineries there welcome visitors. For a listing of all wineries open to visitors, write to the Wine Institute, 717 Market Street, San Francisco, or consult the Sunset book *Wine Country.*

Stockton

Connected to San Francisco Bay by a 76-mile channel, the Port of Stockton is the link between the Bay Area and the rich agricultural and manufacturing areas of the San Joaquin Valley. The docks on the immediate west edge of downtown Stockton serve around 700 cargo vessels a year.

The campus of the University of the Pacific is at Pacific Avenue and Stadium Drive. Its ivy-covered Gothic buildings are surrounded by expansive lawns and tall shade trees.

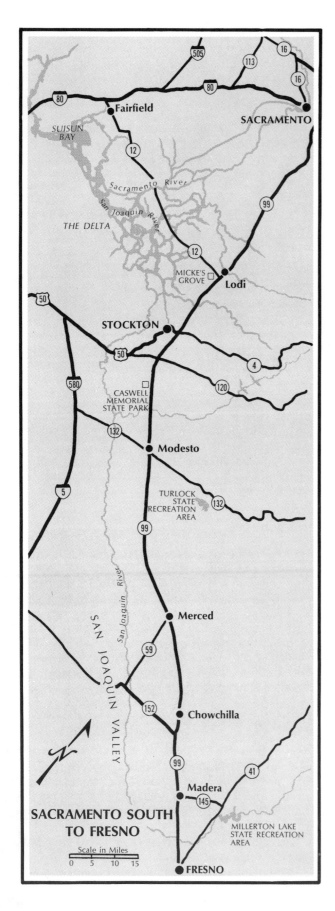

SACRAMENTO SOUTH
TO FRESNO

Scale in Miles
0   5   10   15

Victory Park, at North Pershing Avenue and Acacia Street, offers picnic tables under lofty trees, playground equipment, a duck pond, open spaces, and a museum. In the Pioneer Museum and Haggin Galleries you will find an art collection strong in 19th-century French and American paintings and usually a traveling or local art show. Several rooms depict Indian and pioneer life in the San Joaquin Valley and the history of California. Hours are 1:30 to 5 P.M. Tuesday through Sunday; admission is free.

Pixie Woods, in Louis Park 2 miles west of Stockton, is a children's fantasyland playground, with dragons to climb on, a topsy-turvy house, and a slide down a giraffe's neck. Pixie Woods is open weekends, April through October, from noon to 6 P.M. Between mid-June and mid-September, it is open Wednesday, Thursday, and Friday as well, from noon to 8 P.M. There is a small admission charge.

Caswell Memorial State Park

Sixteen miles south of Stockton and about 5 miles west of State 99, Caswell Memorial State Park contains one of the few remaining groves of valley oaks which once prevailed throughout practically all of the Central Valley.

The park's campsites are especially welcome because of the short supply in the Valley. It is also a pleasant place to picnic and a cool refuge in summer.

In the 258-acre park, 90 acres have remained a primitive area where no natural features will be altered. A mile-long trail under a ceiling of arched branches begins beyond the picnic grounds.

Miller Ranch

An impressive collection of antique vehicles (farm machinery, horse-drawn vehicles, bicycles, tractors, and automobiles) can be seen at the Miller Ranch. The privately-owned ranch, 10 miles east of Modesto at 9425 Yosemite Boulevard, also has antique household items, a general store, a blacksmith shop, and an oldtime barbershop. Admission is 50 cents for adults and 25 cents for children.

Turlock Lake State Recreation Area

You can camp at quiet campsites along the Tuolumne River; or, across the county road that splits this park, you can picnic in either of two picnic areas on Turlock Lake. The park is 23 miles east of Modesto via State Highway 132. On the lake side of the park there are sandy beaches, swimming areas, boat harbor and launching ramps, and a water-ski beach. A concession sells groceries and fishing supplies. Fishing is good in the Tuolumne River, and you can swim in the river during the low-water season.

The Merced area

Three state parks alongside rivers are good places for picnicking, swimming, and fishing. McConnell is a few miles east of State 99 on the south shore of the Merced River, George J. Hatfield, 5 miles east of Newman on the San Joaquin River, and Fremont Ford, between Merced and Gustine on State Highway 140. Two of them—McConnell and George J. Hatfield—have campsites.

Seven miles northeast of Merced, just up into the hills, 400-acre Yosemite Lake is popular for boating, swimming, and shoreline picnicking. The lake is 1½ miles long, with sloping shores ideal for family swimming.

Between Merced and Fresno you'll see hundreds of acres of Thompson Seedless vineyards. When the grapes are picked to make raisins (other uses are for table grapes or for sweet wines), the pickers lay them on pieces of heavy paper between the rows to dry for several weeks. The rows almost always run east and west so the grape-raisins can bask in sun all day. After drying, the raisins go off to plants for cleaning, processing, and packing.

Millerton Lake State Recreation Area

Millerton Lake, 22 miles northeast of Madera, is one of the larger recreation-developed reservoirs in the Valley. There are campgrounds and a new Group Camp (for organized groups) at the north shore (7 miles north of Friant), and the main recreation area of the south bay is a mile from Friant. Boat launching ramps are located at both areas. On the south shore, you will also find a boat and motor rental concession. The lake, about 16 miles long, offers boating, good fishing, and swimming. A boat access camp is 16 miles upstream at Temperance Flat.

In and around Fresno

Seven miles west of Fresno, at 7160 West Eucalyptus Avenue, is the old estate of wealthy land developer M. Theo Kearney. The Edwardian mansion is a museum open to the public from 2 to 5 P.M. Wednesday through Sunday in the summer and Thursday through Sunday October 1 through June 1. The estate and Kearney Boulevard, which leads to it from Fresno, were planted in 1888 with eucalyptus (now towering giants), palms, and oleanders.

In Fresno is 150-acre Roeding Park. A pioneer nurseryman planted this big piece of land with hundreds of trees, including many picturesque eucalyptus. Roeding Park now lies between old U.S.99 on the east and the new State 99 by-pass on the west. It has a children's storyland, a zoo, an amusement playground, boating, tennis courts, and picnic areas.

Downtown Fresno radiates a park-like atmosphere. In the central business district—Fulton Street from Inyo to Tuolumne streets—you can stroll through a mall embellished with trees, flowers, pools, fountains, and modern sculpture.

BEYOND DUCK POND is imposing Pioneer Museum and Haggin Galleries in Stockton's Victory Park. Park also displays tall totem pole.

CONTEMPORARY sculpture is a feature of Fresno's downtown mall.

THE SIERRA NEVADA

Gold Country • Feather River • Lake Tahoe
Yosemite • Wilderness Areas

Yosemite Valley

The Sierra Nevada is the largest single mountain range in the country. It rises gradually from the floor of the Central Valley, ascending in 60 to 90 miles to a jagged crest that runs from 7,000 to 14,000 feet in altitude, and then plunges down a mile to the desert-like Owens Valley to the east.

Evidence of glacial action is visible in many areas. Nearly every deep-cut valley owes its present configuration to glacial abrasion. Best known example of the power of the glacier is Yosemite Valley, which was formed by the cutting action of slow-moving ice during the Ice Age.

The higher elevations of the Sierra offer fishing in mountain streams, boating and water-skiing on Lake Tahoe, hiking trails into primitive areas, and awe-inspiring scenery at Yosemite. The Sierra foothills are also a drawing card—rich in remnants and relics from the bustling Gold Rush days.

GOLD COUNTRY

The Gold Rush Country of the Sierra Nevada foothills ranges from rolling grassland a few hundred feet above sea level to the 6,700-foot elevation of fir-clad, often snowy Yuba Pass. State Highway 49 runs through the heart of this country. It stays at around 2,000 feet, except where it dips into deep river canyons and climbs mountains above Downieville.

In the summer, weather is likely to be hot at the lower altitudes but pleasant in the pine belt at higher levels. The dust probably will be deep on the unpaved logging roads as it was along the thoroughfares traveled by the coaches of the Central Overland Stage in the 1850's. But when fall arrives rains come to settle the dust and to brighten the old towns with yellow and vermilion.

Winter rains turn the red foothill soil to mud, and snow covers the higher altitudes. At the lower elevations, spring comes in February and March. In April and May, some mountain towns may still have some snow and the back roads might be deep with mud, but the rest of the foothills are covered with wildflowers and spring grass.

Gold Country has plenty of comfortable, up-to-date hotels and motels, and a few old inns are open to guests (see page 105). Reservations are advisable in the summer. Camping is impractical if not impossible at the lower elevations in summer; the privately owned, tinder-dry grasslands are fenced and posted. Heading east from State 49, though, you will reach Forest Service campgrounds at the higher, cooler levels.

Here some of the main points of interest in the major towns along State 49 are discussed. For more detailed descriptions of these and other towns of the Gold Country, and for some of its history and legends, refer to the Sunset Book *Gold Rush Country*.

Old Columbia's main street

Emerald Bay

Mariposa country

Mariposa is the southernmost Gold Rush town and about the southernmost point of State 49. Here you can see the oldest courthouse in California. This two-story wooden structure, situated on a quiet hill at the north end of town, has been in use continuously since it was built in 1854, and the clock in its square tower has rung the hours since it was installed in 1866. One block east of the main street is the 30 by 50-foot granite block structure, once the largest jail in the entire Mother Lode.

First village north of Mariposa is Mount Bullion, where the now-vanished Princeton Mine produced more than $4,000,000 in gold.

A 13-mile side trip west from Mount Bullion on Old Toll Road will take you to Hornitos, where many charming old buildings frame a Mexican-style plaza. At High Street and Bear Valley Road is the entrance to an escape tunnel through which the Mother Lode's most famous badman, Joaquin Murieta, retreated from the fandango hall. A noticeable ruin is the Ghirardelli Store—it was in this building that the man who was to accumulate a fortune in chocolate began to build his business empire.

Proceeding north on State 49, you will come to Bear Valley, the town John Fremont once "owned." Here is the Bon Ton Saloon, roofless jail, Garbarino Store, local Odd Fellows Hall and Trabucco Store.

Coulterville, north of Bear Valley, has the old Jeffery Hotel built in 1851 of rock and adobe. The walls are three feet thick. Across the street are the remains of the Coulter Hotel and the Wells Fargo Building.

A side trip west from Coulterville on State Highway 132 will take you to La Grange on the bank of the Tuolumne River. Once a stopping place for three major stage lines, La Grange now has few remnants of the Gold Rush days—an old adobe post office and the wooden Odd Fellows Hall.

In and around Sonora

Sonora is as bustling today as it was a century ago. It is the county seat of Tuolumne County and a trading center for the surrounding cattle and lumber country. Modern facades cover the aged buildings which line Washington Street, and traffic moves slowly along the crowded thoroughfare. But a drive off the main street half a block will take you back to Gold Rush days. Sonora's outstanding piece of old architecture is St. James Episcopal Church on Washington Street at the north end of town. Built in 1860, the graceful structure is said to be the Gold Country's most beautiful frame building.

South of Sonora on State 49 is Jamestown. A few old balconied buildings on its main street date back to the 1870's. Chinese Camp, farther south, was

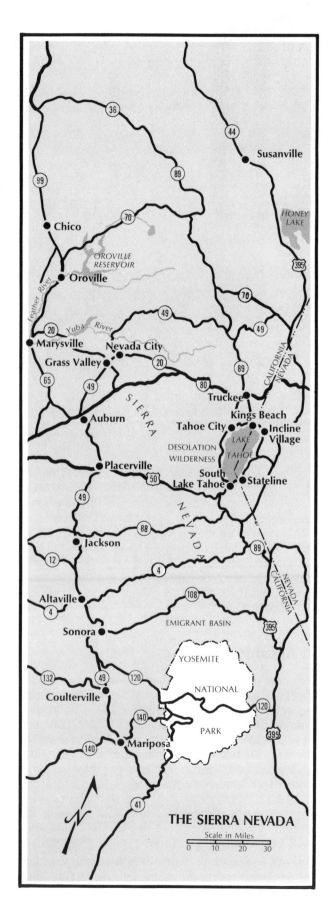

THE SIERRA NEVADA

Scale in Miles

0   10   20   30

named for the thousands of Chinese who mined the area in the early 1850's.

Four miles north of Sonora sits Columbia, "Gem of the Southern Mines." This town, which is today maintained as a state historic park, was one of the most important settlements in the Mother Lode and is the most carefully preserved.

Youngsters can pan for gold down in Matelot Gulch or ride a jouncing stagecoach (which leaves from the Express Office) through the granite-ribbed hills behind town. They can sip a sarsaparilla at the old State Drivers Retreat saloon, get a haircut at the oldest barbershop in the state, or sit down to a platter of Hangtown Fry or some forty-niner delicacy amidst the turn-of-the-century elegance of Columbia House Restaurant.

Main Street also offers shops selling miner's rock crystal candy, gold pans, leather goods, western clothing, and Gold Country souvenirs. There are old freight wagons to climb upon and rocky grottoes in Matelot Gulch to explore. A museum displays gold nuggets.

There is also the old ice depot with great 100-pound blocks of ice stacked neatly in sawdust; the corner grocery with its glass-fronted bins, and the old confectionery with its marbletopped counter.

A side trip north on State Highway 4 will take you through the old camps of Vallecito and Douglas Flat to Murphys. Most prominent of Murphys' old buildings is the Murphys Hotel built in 1855. You can examine the old register and find names of illustrious travelers of the past—Mark Twain, U. S. Grant, Henry Ward Beecher, J. Pierpont Morgan, Horatio Alger, and many others.

If you take State 49 from Columbia you will pass through Jackass Hill, where Mark Twain's cabin is reconstructed on its original site. In Tuttletown are the ruins of Swerer's store, which both Mark Twain and Bret Harte frequented. At the south end of Carson Hill is the yawning slash of the Morgan Mine on the hill above town. Fifteen miles of tunnel run through the hill, and one of the shafts reaches down almost 5,000 feet.

Angels Camp, north of Carson Hill, was made famous by Mark Twain's tale "The Celebrated Jumping Frog of Calaveras County." The story set in Angels Camp is commemorated every year in May with a Jumping Frog Jubilee. In a shady park along State 49 is an imposing statue of Mark Twain and along the main street is a monument to the frog. Well-kept old homes comprise the residential sections of Angels Camp. Interesting old buildings include the green and white Peirano Building, the Angels Hotel, and the imposing jailhouse behind it.

In Altaville, north of Angels Camp, is the handsome Prince and Garibardi Store—a two-story stone building erected over a century ago. An old iron foundry is also located here.

GRAVEMARKERS reveal violence and tragic incidents of Gold Rush history to fascinated youngsters.

COLUMBIA'S STAGECOACH leaves from Express Office. Riders have choice of coach or shotgun seat.

The Jackson area

Jackson, a town that has kept up with progress, is also trying to preserve its 19th-century heritage. Modern facades have transformed many of the old buildings along the main street, but a walk along the side streets will reveal some of the flavor of the past.

One of the most interesting buildings in town is the Brown House, built in the 1860's on a hill about 2 blocks east of the main part of town. Today it serves as the county museum. On the narrow main street are the Odd Fellows Hall and the restored National Hotel. St. Sava's Serbian Orthodox Church, built in 1893, is unusual for its European architectural style.

For many decades two great hard-rock mines, the Kennedy and the Argonaut, were very important in Jackson's economy, but neither has been worked in many years. The huge tailing wheels built at the Kennedy Mine in 1912 are still standing and can be seen from State 49. For a closer view drive the Jackson Gate road out on State Highway 88 and hike along the well-marked trails.

Volcano, a side trip of about 12 miles east from Jackson on Volcano Road, has many remains of the early town—the St. George Hotel, the old jail, a brewery built in 1856, the Odd Fellows-Masonic Hall, the Adams Express Office, and the Lavezzo Building.

Sutter Creek and Amador City, 3 miles north of Jackson on State 49, were important quartz mining centers. As in many Gold Country towns, their side streets are the most interesting to explore. The museum in Amador City has an interesting collection of Gold Rush relics.

South of Jackson on State 49 is Mokelumne Hill. Many of its buildings are built of light brown stone (rhyolite tuff), a material common to much of the Mother Lode. The Odd Fellows Hall was the first three-story building in the Gold Country. You can also see the remains of the Meyer Store and the famous old Leger Hotel with its elegant balconies. The Congregational Church, built in 1856, sits on columns of fitted stone blocks.

From Placerville to Grass Valley

Placerville, county seat of El Dorado County, was one of the great camps of the Gold Country. Founded in 1848, it was originally called Dry Diggings, because the miners had to cart the dry soil down to running

SUTTER'S MILL, reconstructed in Coloma, is where gold dust was first discovered in 1848.

The Auburn-Forest Hill Road leaves State 49 east of Auburn and winds into the hills along the route of an old turnpike to the lumber town of Forest Hill, where one of the best-preserved hydraulic nozzles in Gold Country is on display. Beyond Forest Hill is Michigan Bluff, where extensive hydraulic mining took place.

You can take other side trips into former mining camps by following some of the country roads that exit east off Interstate 80 around Colfax.

Between Grass Valley and Sierra City

A disastrous fire in 1855 destroyed the early community of Grass Valley, and there is little left to recall the town's mining camp days. But Grass Valley still has its narrow streets and a few old structures such as the cottage of Lola Montez, whose daring behavior made her the talk of Europe and America. Once a year the Grass Valley-Nevada City Kiwanis Club offers a tour of the quartz mines in the area. The tour, which takes a good part of the day, includes visits to at least five mines, the Big Pelton Wheel (which spun around at 70 miles an hour to produce power), and the Malakoff Diggin's (where hydraulic mining scars mark the San Juan Ridge).

Five miles north of Grass Valley, Nevada City sits on the banks of Deer Creek. Once Nevada City was one of the most picturesque Gold Rush towns, but a recent freeway has destroyed some of its gracious elegance. Residential sections contain many gabled frame houses, and the downtown area has a number of historical buildings: the Ott Assay Office, where ore from the Comstock Lode was first analyzed and found rich in silver; the National Hotel, with its balconies and balustrades reaching out over the sidewalk; and the red brick Firehouse #2, now a museum with a collection of remnants of Gold Rush days.

For further exploration follow some of the side roads from Grass Valley and Nevada City. You can reach the old high-country camps of Goodyears Bar, Forest, and Alleghany by turning south off State 49 on the Mountain House Road 3 miles west of Downieville.

Fire and flood have done their best to destroy the mountain settlement of Downieville, but it is still one of the most entrancing gold towns left. The old stone, brick, and frame buildings, many of which were built in the 1860's or earlier, face on quiet, crooked streets and cling to the mountainsides above the Yuba River.

The towering, jagged Sierra Buttes, visible for many miles in all directions, overshadow the half-ghost town of Sierra City. Between 1850 and 1852, Sierra City miners tunneled through these dramatic granite peaks in their search for gold-bearing rock. There are several structures of an early vintage in Sierra City—the biggest is Busch Building, two stories of brick and a third of lumber, built in 1871.

water to wash out the gold. The next year some grisly lynchings gave the town a new name—Hangtown. In 1854 it became Placerville, a bow to self-conscious pride.

In Placerville's main district is the Pony Express Building at 10 Sacramento, originally a harness shop built in 1858. A Pony Express historical marker is in the alley behind the building. The Old City Hall was built in 1857 and the building next door in 1862. The Odd Fellows Hall has been in use since 1859.

Coloma, north of Placerville on State 49, is where gold was first discovered by James Marshall on John Sutter's land. The town is now preserved as a state park, and here you will see Sutter's Mill reconstructed exactly to match the original. On the hill behind town is a bronze statue of Marshall and down the road from the statue is the cabin where he lived in 1868.

Farther north on State 49, the modern city of Auburn is on top of a hill, leaving the old town lying below and west of the imposing county courthouse. To see the brick and stone structures built in the 1850's and 1860's, walk along Lincoln Way and Court and Commercial streets. You will see the round-fronted brick Union Bar; the little frame Joss House, distinguished only by the plank with foot-high incised Chinese characters above the door; the square, four-story firehouse; the Wells Fargo Office, now a gift shop; and the post office.

THE OLD INNS ON HIGHWAY 49

Mellow old inns scattered throughout the Mother Lode country offer a warm welcome for travelers and serve as bases for exploring the countryside.

Some of the hostelries have been in operation for more than a century, others are historic buildings more recently converted to accommodate guests, and one is a replica of a hotel active in Gold Rush times. Accommodations may range from rusticity to Victorian opulence, but all the innkeepers work hard to preserve the feeling of old-fashioned hospitality.

Reservations are always advisable; some hotels close for brief periods during the year. Some of the inns serve meals, some only breakfast, while others have to send guests "down the street" for their meals.

The following inns are in towns on State Highway 49. Rates for double occupancy range from about $6 to $22.50 a night.

● Nevada City. National Hotel: elegant rooms, private baths, attractive dining room. Red Castle: once private residence; morning coffee and afternoon tea included.

● Coloma. Sierra Nevada House III: well appointed replica of an old-timer; soda fountain and restaurant.

● Amador City. Mine House: formerly Keystone Mine offices; morning coffee and juice.

● Sutter Creek. Sutter Creek Inn: intimate, delightful rooms, children not encouraged; big breakfast served. Bellotti Inn: 28 rooms, many furnished with Gold Rush antiques.

● Jackson. National Hotel: old-fashioned saloon entrance with rooms upstairs.

● Mokelumne Hill. Hotel Leger: spacious well decorated rooms, some private baths; two dining rooms.

● Sonora. Gunn House: two-story adobe, redone to combine Victoriana with modern conveniences.

● Coulterville. Jeffery Hotel: museum is primary interest; old rooms.

Red Castle, Nevada City

Sierra Nevada III, Coloma

Gunn House, Sonora

Sutter Creek Inn

Hotel Leger, Mokelumne Hill

MIDDLE FORK of Feather River flows through canyons where some walls tower 5,000 feet above the white water.

FEATHER RIVER COUNTRY

The Feather River Country is rich in scenery and history. Its topography consists of rocky canyons and fern-filled ravines, high mountains, leaf-covered foothills and chaparral slopes, second-growth pine and fir forests. And through all this flows the Feather River.

Three major waterways form the Feather River: North Fork, Middle Fork, and South Fork. A lesser one flowing into the North Fork is the West Branch. State Highway 70 follows the North Fork of the Feather and affords panoramic views of the canyon country. The Middle Fork, the most rugged, offers some of the finest trout fishing in California. The South Fork, site of many early placer mining locations, has many swimming holes and hiking trails. Along its stretches are seven reservoir lakes—the highest at 5,000 feet is the 500-acre Grass Valley Lake.

The Feather River acquired its name from the Spanish explorer Don Luis Arguello in 1820. He reached the lower Feather during the band-tailed pigeon migration and dubbed it El Rio de las Plumas for the feathers floating in it.

There were Indians in this region—the Maidu—a self-sufficient mountain and foothill people who hunted deer with bow and arrow, speared salmon and steelhead, and searched the hillsides for acorns, roots, and herbs. But the Feather River was the site of major gold strikes (Bidwells Bar, gold discovery site, is now under 450 feet of water), and by 1860 the Indian way of life had been destroyed by the hordes of gold seekers from the East.

The Feather River Highway, State Highway 70, connects the Central Valley and the Sierra. It follows the deep canyon of the North Fork, touches the edges of the upper Middle Fork, crosses nine bridges, and tunnels through three masses of solid granite.

Along most of this route there are a number of Forest Service campgrounds, major resorts, and cabin settlements. Most stretches along the way are heavily fished. Stub roads lead off to old mining settlements, to little pocket valleys that have been cultivated since 1850, and to trout-filled lakes beneath granite domes. Trails take off where roads end.

Oroville

Oroville, 75 miles north of Sacramento on State 70, is the gateway to the Feather River Country. Today a lumber processing center and the center of an extensive olive-growing area, Oroville first sprang up as Ophir City—a boisterous tent town of Gold Rush days. In the 1870's, when thousands of Chinese worked the diggings in the area, Oroville had a Chinatown that was the largest in California.

Oroville's richest reminder of the past is the Chinese Temple, now a museum of Oriental artifacts, at

TWO FIERCE WARRIORS *are part of the tapestry collection in Oroville's Chinese Temple.*

HOME *of Charles F. Lott, circuit judge and state senator, has period pieces, old-fashioned gardens.*

Broderick Street behind the levee of the Feather River. Recently added to the original structure—built in 1863—is the Tapestry Hall, connected to the temple by an open courtyard and garden with a graceful copper pagoda and small reflecting pool surrounded by Chinese plantings. At the entrance to the temple is a 2-ton brass incense burner said to have been the gift of the Emperor Quong She of the Ching Dynasty. You can visit the temple from 10 A.M. to 12 noon, 1 to 4 P.M. Friday through Tuesday, 1 to 5 P.M. Wednesday and Thursday.

Another Oroville landmark is the Judge C. F. Lott Memorial Home in Sank Park. The white frame dwelling, completed in 1856, is furnished with period pieces and sits among landscaped gardens. The house is open Wednesday through Sunday from 10:30 A.M. to 4 P.M., Monday and Tuesday by appointment; June 1 to October 15 daily. From December 1 to January 15 the house is closed. A broad patio, a recent addition, is the site of Sunday afternoon programs during the spring and summer months.

Oroville Dam

Five and a half miles northeast of Oroville, on the Feather River, is the Oroville Dam. Towering 770 feet above metropolitan Oroville, it is the highest dam in the United States and the highest earth fill dam in the world.

Oroville Dam serves many purposes. Much of the water stored in Lake Oroville, behind the dam, is diverted into a system of aqueducts, tunnels, and basins which extend the length of California. Adjoining the dam in the Feather River Canyon wall is a powerhouse which can generate enough electricity to support a city of one million people. The dam offers a large measure of protection against river floods. A state recreation area around the lake affords a variety of outdoor activities.

Lake Oroville

Lake Oroville, with a surface area of about 15,800 acres and about 167 miles of shoreline, has been designated a state recreation area. Boating, water-skiing, swimming, fishing, and sailing are the most popular activities. Picnicking and camping facilities are available. There are also reserved areas for boat-in camping and houseboat mooring.

At the park's visitor center are interpretive displays and statistical information about the dam and the lake. An observation area affords a panoramic view

SPECTACULAR SCENERY surrounds Lake Oroville, a recreation area created by Oroville Dam project. Dam is highest in United States and is a key unit in California water system.

of Lake Oroville on one side and Oroville and the remainder of the vast water project on the other side. For information about recreational activities, write to Oroville Reservoir State Recreation Area, 400 Glen Drive, Oroville, California 95965.

Across the Middle Fork arm of Lake Oroville is the Bidwell Bar Bridge. The suspension bridge, 627 feet above the river bed before the lake was full, now is only 70 feet above water.

Feather Falls and Bald Rock Canyon

The Feather Falls Scenic Area is a 14,890-acre preserve of forested canyons, soaring granite domes, and plunging waterfalls in a remote section of Plumas National Forest just north and slightly east of Lake Oroville. Set aside by the Forest Service to preserve the special qualities of this particular segment of the Feather River drainage, the scenic area includes Feather Falls and Bald Rock Canyon.

Feather Falls, a plume-like cascade of the Fall River plunging 640 feet in a single leap, lends its name to the scenic area. The easiest way to see the falls is by boating to the end of the Middle Fork arm of Lake Oroville and then climbing a half-mile trail.

By inland route, take the Oroville-Quincy Road to Forbestown Road to Lumpkin Road. Six miles beyond Feather Falls on the Lumpkin-La Porte Road is the rough Frey Ranch Road which loops northwest about 4 miles to a trail head. It is a 2-mile hike from the end of this road to the brink of the falls.

There are scenic viewpoints along the Bald Rock Dome canyon rim; however, the canyon floor is primitive and inaccessible. The Milsap Bar Road crosses the Middle Fork at the upper end of the canyon, but there is not even a foot trail to its inner depths.

To reach the Milsap Bar Bridge from Lake Oroville, follow the Oroville-Quincy Highway north for about 16 miles (via Berry Creek) to the Brush Creek Ranger Station. Then head east on the Milsap Bar Road about 7 miles to the river crossing.

Bucks Lake

Bucks Lake, formed in 1924 when Bucks Creek was dammed, is nestled in the Feather River country at a mile-high elevation. To reach the lake, follow the Feather River Highway (State 70) to Quincy, then turn west on the paved 17-mile road to Bucks Lake. The lake can also be approached from Oroville via the Oroville-Quincy and the Spanish Ranch roads.

The south shore of the lake is a resort area where boating (rentals are available), swimming, water-skiing, and fishing are prime attractions. Forest Service and private campgrounds are also located here. If you prefer wilderness camping, cross the lake to the roadless north shore where there are a number of excellent camping and fishing spots.

Hikers and horsemen can reach 10 other lakes and numerous streams scattered through the back country. Good fishing destinations are Bear Creek, Grizzly Creek, and the Middle Fork of the Feather, reached on foot, by horseback, or by jeep.

At nearby Lower Bucks Lake, there is good fishing for rainbows and browns. You can find undeveloped campsites on the north side of this lake, too. Access is over a dirt road from the Bucks Lake south shore.

UPPER YUBA RECREATION AREAS

Thousands of acres of forested land in the Plumas and Tahoe national forests offer trout fishing or swimming in mountain streams, camping in secluded spots, hiking or horseback riding, hunting, and skiing. Interstate highways 70 and 80 and state highways 49 and 89 are the main routes through the forests. Much of the Plumas National Forest is in Feather River country, while Tahoe National Forest extends south and east to the Nevada border. For a detailed map of roads, trails, campsites, and lakes, write to either Plumas National Forest, Quincy, California 95971, or to Tahoe National Forest, Nevada City, California 95959.

Lakes Basin and Sierra Buttes recreation areas

To reach Lakes Basin and Sierra Buttes, turn off State 89 on to Gold Lake Road at Graeagle, just southeast of Blairsden. You can also approach this area from State 49. Turn north several miles east of Sierra City at Gold Lake Road.

The Basin itself is only 12 miles long and 5 miles wide. It extends from Mount Elwell (7,812 feet) at the northern end to the craggy Sierra Buttes (8,587 feet) at the southern end. Unusual glacial activity has left its mark: a haphazard jumble of slopes holding some 40 lake bowls gouged out of the polished, sparsely forested granite.

A low divide separates the Basin geographically into two areas. Creeks and lakes in the northern section (Lakes Basin) form an important source of the Feather River, and those in the southern part (Sierra Buttes) drain into the Yuba. These lakes offer good trout fishing, and some boating and swimming. The usual camping season is June through October, but it depends on the snow melt. Roads are normally passable in June. Summer days are warm, but the

TROUT *caught in mountain stream in Tahoe National Forest serve as dinner for Sierra campers.*

nights are cold. Winds can make tent camping difficult, especially around Gold Lake.

Three small Forest Service campgrounds are in the southern section at Snag Lake, Salmon Creek, and Lower Sardine Lake. Resorts are at Salmon, Sardine, and Packer lakes. In the northern section, there is a campground at Lakes Basin and at Grassy Lake. There are also Forest Service camps near Blairsden and on State 49 near Sierra City.

Plumas-Eureka State Park and Jamison Lakes

On the slopes of Eureka Peak, surrounded by Plumas forest land, is the 4,000-acre Plumas-Eureka State Park. You enter the park through Johnsville on the Johnsville-McRae Meadows Road. There are hiking trails (many of them roads from mining days) on Eureka Peak and on Mt. Elwell and Mt. Washington to the south. Picnic facilities are available, and there is a campground on Upper Jamison Creek. Trout fishing is excellent at Eureka and Madora lakes and in the numerous mountain streams.

The old mining town of Johnsville and the Plumas-Eureka stamp mill within the park recall the gold

EMERALD BAY, bounded by two state parks, is inlet on Lake Tahoe's southwest shore. High road here provides best views of lake.

PLACID lakefront attracts visitors to South Lake Tahoe City Beach.

mining days. A mining history museum is open the year around.

Plumas-Eureka State Park is open the year around. After October 1, the campground closes; however, the museum and the park headquarters remain open throughout the year. Eureka Bowl is open for skiing, with a ski-lift operating on Wednesday, Saturday, and Sunday.

Just a few miles from the main road of the Plumas-Eureka State Park are the Jamison Lakes. All four lakes (Jamison, Grass, Wades, and Rock) are glacial excavations in a high valley below McRae Ridge, bound on the east by Mt. Elwell and on the west by Mt. Washington.

Jamison and Grass lakes offer the best fishing, with large populations of rainbow and eastern brook trout. Peak fishing is just after the ice melts (usually by the middle of June) and again in September. Several short hiking trails connect the lakes.

LAKE TAHOE

Between the two main emigrant routes of California's early settlers (now U.S. Highway 50 and Interstate 80) lies Lake Tahoe, an extremely popular vacation area. Surrounded by the heavily timbered Sierra Nevada, a brilliantly clear, unbelievably blue Lake Tahoe offers both summer and winter activities.

Boating, swimming (the water is cold), and water-skiing are the main summer activities. Skiing is the prime winter attraction. As Lake Tahoe does not freeze over, you can fish the year around.

Lake Tahoe is 22 miles long and 8 to 12 miles wide. You can drive around the lake on a 71-mile shoreline drive that offers excellent views of the lake's clear waters, the many coves, and the sheer mountain sides that plummet into the lake. This drive is recommended only during the summer, as winter snows close a section of U.S. Highway 89 between Tahoe City and Tahoe Valley.

Many people prefer to visit Lake Tahoe in the spring or fall, before the seasonal crowds arrive. However, during the off-season the weather is unpredictable. Snow can fall from October to June. If you visit Tahoe during the winter, you should carry car chains. Blizzard conditions can make mountain driving hazardous.

A variety of accommodations is available at Tahoe. You have your choice of resorts, motels, campgrounds (summer only), or private cabins. For information concerning south shore accommodations and recreational facilities, write to South Lake Tahoe Chamber of Commerce, Box 3418, South Lake Tahoe, California 95705. For information concerning the north

VIKINGSHOLM, hidden at southern tip of Emerald Bay, is exact replica of Norseman fortress of 800 A.D.

MOOR your boat to this pier on Emerald Bay and picnic before or after your visit to Vikingsholm.

shore, write to the Greater North Lake Tahoe Chamber of Commerce, Box 884, Tahoe City, California 95730. Reservations are advisable.

Part of Lake Tahoe is in Nevada. On the Nevada side of the lake are gambling establishments which operate around the clock during the summer. During the winter months most of the larger ones stay open for skiers and other winter sports enthusiasts. The principal gambling areas are at Stateline at the south shore and Crystal Bay and Incline Village at the north shore.

Recreation on and around the lake

Lake Tahoe is a mecca for boaters and water-skiers. There is plenty of room for everyone, and the many coves and harbors along the lake's shore are appealing. There are many places where you can rent boats, or if you have your own boat there are plenty of launching ramps. During the heavy summer season, you may have trouble finding a mooring. If a summer thunderstorm appears imminent, do not venture too far from shore, as the lake can become very rough. Because of the winds and vast size of the lake, sailing and canoeing are not common.

Swimmers unaffected by the cold water will find plenty of public beaches. At the south end of the lake are three forest service beaches (Pope, Baldwin, and Kiva). There is also swimming at D. L. Bliss and Emerald Bay state parks and Tahoe State Recreation Area and on the Nevada side at Sand Harbor Beach Recreation Area and Zephyr Cove. Many boat harbors also have beaches.

Rainbow, Mackinaw, silver, brown, eastern brook, and cutthroat trout can be taken from the lake. Fishing licenses from California and Nevada are usable anywhere on the lake, but only if you depart from and return to the state issuing the license. In the many lakes and streams close to Tahoe, you can trout fish from May to October.

Around Tahoe there are many excellent hiking trails. Inquire locally for the best trips. The Forest Service also publishes maps for hikers.

The country surrounding Lake Tahoe is ideal for winter sports. Eight miles from Tahoe City, off State Highway 89, is Squaw Valley. A mile south of the Squaw Valley turnoff is the road to Alpine Meadows ski area (3 miles from the highway). At the south end of the lake near Bijou is Heavenly Valley with an enclosed aerial tramway that rises to 8,300 feet, affording beautiful views of the lake. On the north shore are Incline Village, Mt. Rose, and Slide Mountain. Main roads are usually open throughout the year, but check on local conditions before you start out.

The South Shore

Lake Tahoe's south shore is more heavily populated than the north shore. Resorts, motels, and private cabins are plentiful, there are number of public beaches, and Nevada's Stateline offers gambling excitement and nightclub entertainment. To reach the south shore, take State Highway 50 from Sacramento or state highways 88 and 89 from Stockton. Scheduled and charter airlines fly into Tahoe from the San Francisco and Los Angeles areas, and from Reno and Stockton.

At the southwestern tip of the lake is Tahoe's greatest scenic attraction, Emerald Bay. The bay is entirely within Bliss and Emerald Bay state parks, and its waters surround Tahoe's only island, Emerald Isle. The road around Emerald Bay is high above the water, and the view is unparalleled anywhere else on the lake.

Unseen from the road, at the southern tip of the bay, is a 38-room castle, called *Vikingsholm*, once a summer residence. A striking example of Scandinavian architecture, Vikingsholm was patterned after a Norseman fortress of 800 A.D. During the summer, the house is open to visitors daily. Park your car at Inspiration Point and then hike about a mile to Vikingsholm.

South of Emerald Bay are several forest service beaches. The El Dorado National Forest Visitors Center, on State Highway 89 north of Camp Richardson, offers slide presentations, group campfires at the Lake of the Sky Amphitheater, guided half-day walks into the Desolation Valley Primitive Area, lecture programs at Angora Ridge fire lookout station, boat tours of Echo Lake, and short walks through surrounding meadows. There is also a stream profile chamber containing a series of living dioramas along an artificially created bypass of Taylor Creek, a natural trout and salmon spawning stream that flows from Fallen Leaf Lake to enter Lake Tahoe at Camp Richardson. The center is open from 9 A.M. to 6 P.M. daily June 21 through September 21.

The South Lake Tahoe City Beach, on Lakeshore Boulevard, offers water-skiing and swimming. Picnic fires and overnight camping are prohibited on the beach, but there are approximately 350 campsites available within walking distance at the South Lake Tahoe El Dorado Recreational Area.

The major south shore ski area is Heavenly Valley. The turnoff is just beyond Bijou. South of Meyers on U.S. 50 are Sierra Ski Ranch and Echo Summit Ski Area.

The North Shore

The state line is the high point of activity for the north shore. Here, the motels, lodges, cabins, and

WINTER brings thousands of ski enthusiasts to Tahoe. Here skiers try jump slope at Squaw Valley.

gambling casinos crowd State Highway 28 on either side. Once you cross into California, the casinos disappear, but the towns of Brockway, Kings Beach, and Tahoe Vista are fused to form a solid resort area.

Nevada's Incline Village is a good family ski area. (Farther north on Nevada Highway 27 is the Mt. Rose Ski Area and Slide Mountain.) Also at Incline Village is a golf course and the Ponderosa Ranch where location scenes for TV's Bonanza are filmed.

On the California side, a pine-forested area between Carnelian Bay and Tahoe City is relatively undeveloped. Tahoe City has a golf course and a public beach and is a stopping place for Squaw Valley and Alpine Meadows skiers. North of Tahoe City is a state recreation area.

To reach the north shore, take Interstate 80 to State 89 for Tahoe City or to State Highway 267 for Kings Beach. Airports are located at Truckee and Reno.

Squaw Valley State Recreation Area

Eight miles south of Truckee, a 2-mile side road from State 89 leads into Squaw Valley State Recreation Area, locale of the 1960 Winter Olympics. When the Olympics were concluded, the state of California fell heir to 1,029 acres of the site for use as a park.

Family-type accommodations and meals are available at the state-owned Olympic Village (originally constructed as dormitories for the Olympic contestants). Facilities include an ice-skating rink at Blythe Arena, a heated all-year swimming pool, and two spectator centers where you can watch the activity on the slopes. Picnicking is permitted in the park, but there are no camping facilities.

Adjacent to but not included in the state property are two privately owned resorts, Squaw Valley Inn and Squaw Valley Lodge.

Donner Memorial State Park and Donner Lake

Just two miles west of Truckee via Interstate 80, Donner Memorial State Park is a popular recreation area alongside Donner Lake. The park stands as a memorial to the members of the ill-fated Donner Party who camped here during the winter of 1846-47. Forty-two of the 89 persons in the party perished in the severe Sierra winter cold and heavy snows. A monument stands in the park on the site of the Brien family shack. Its stone base stands 22 feet high, the depth of snow during that fateful winter.

The Emigrant Trail Museum in the park displays Indian and Donner Party relics. On display near the museum is a steam trailer which once hauled cut lumber on the eastern slope of the Sierra. Most of the park's trails begin at the museum.

CRAG LAKE, in densely forested valley of Desolation Wilderness, supports healthy population of trout.

DESOLATION WILDERNESS

Just over the ridge along Lake Tahoe's southwest shore is Desolation Wilderness, a favorite of Sierra connoisseurs. The best time of year here is between July 15 and October 1. September is a good month—crowds have thinned out and the air is autumn crisp. Snow usually begins to fall in November, and the wilderness becomes inaccessible.

As its name implies, the area is wild and lonely, glistening with glacier-polished granite slopes and huge boulders, and nearly devoid of trees. But there are also forests of fir, pine, hemlock, juniper, and aspens, and Sierra meadows where the wildflowers are colorful in the spring. There are about 70 named lakes in the wilderness, good for trout fishing. Most people find the water too cold for swimming.

Within Desolation Wilderness' 63,469 acres, there are about 50 miles of trails with 5 major trail entrances to choose from. The Tahoe-Yosemite trail is much used and connects many lakes. Backpack trips are extremely popular, or if you prefer, stock trips (animal carry the supplies).

For information on backpacking or wilderness trips, write to District Ranger, U.S. Forest Service, P.O. Box 8465, South Lake Tahoe, California 95705 or Pollock Pines, California 95726.

POWELL LAKE, at 8,800 feet, is one of about 100 lakes in Emigrant Basin which offers fishing. You hike into this primitive area—trails connect points of entry and lakes.

EMIGRANT BASIN

Emigrant Basin Primitive Area, just north of Yosemite National Park, offers green meadows, patches of pine forests, good trout waters, and massive granite peaks. Nearest main highway is State 108—from which short stub roads lead to trail heads.

Emigrant Basin covers 97,000 acres—all within the Stanislaus National Forest. Elevations range from 5,200 feet near Cherry Lake at the south to 11,570 feet at Leavitt Peak at the northeast corner. Snow blankets the area from mid-October until June, with snow covering some sections the year around. Summer temperatures fluctuate—from 90 degrees during the day to below freezing at night.

The area was named for a party of emigrants who were seeking a shortcut over the Sierra Nevada. Several relics which recall the early days are a headstone marking the grave of one pioneer who died in 1853 near Summit Creek and a broken rim of a wagon wheel at Relief Creek.

There are about 100 lakes in Emigrant Basin which offer trout fishing. Some of the larger lakes—Huckleberry, Emigrant, and Long—are more than 100 acres in size. This primitive area also has 142 miles of trails which connect various points of entry with lakes, streams, and campsites. There are no improved campgrounds; however, some of the heavily used sites such as Emigrant Lake, Cow Meadow, and Bucks Lake have log tables and sanitation facilities. In most of the basin you will find plenty of wood and water.

YOSEMITE NATIONAL PARK

The 7-mile Yosemite Valley is neither the deepest nor the longest phenomenon of its kind in the Sierra, but of all the glacial gorges it exhibits the sheerest walls, the most distinctive monoliths, the flattest floor, the widest meadows, and the finest array of waterfalls.

The floor of the valley is a level meadow-like tract threaded by a dashing mountain stream (the Merced River) and diversified with groves of pines, oaks, thickets of smaller growth, and beautiful varieties of flowers, ferns, and grasses.

The walls of the valley rise, almost vertically, to a height of 2,000 to 4,000 feet above the meadow. Great domes and pinnacles stand out against the sky. Most conspicuous are El Capitan, Cathedral Rocks, Three Brothers, North Dome, and Half Dome. Rushing waterfalls tumble from the cliffs, each with its own particular beauty.

Above Yosemite Valley lie almost 1,200 square miles of towering peaks, rugged canyons, high mountain passes, and countless streams, lakes, and waterfalls. The high country offers summer hiking and packing trips at Tuolumne Meadows and the High Sierra camps, and resort facilities at Wawona.

The best time to visit Yosemite is before Memorial Day or after Labor Day. June, July, and August are the valley's busiest months, with campers filling the park nightly. However, restrictions on the number and the time limit of campsites have helped to relieve the congestion. If you visit Yosemite during the summer and want to escape the crowds, plan to take trail trips into the high country.

You can reach Yosemite via Manteca or Modesto on State Highway 120 or via Merced on State Highway 140. From Southern California take State Highway 41 from Fresno. You can enter from the east side of the park over State 120 and Tioga Pass only during the summer when the road is clear of snow.

Where to stay

You have your choice of accommodations—from canvas tents to rustic cabins to hotel-type rooms.

In the valley, Camp Curry, open from late May to early September, has tent cabins and redwood cabins with or without bath (the latter are available the year around). Yosemite Lodge offers complete, all-year facilities. There are hotel-type rooms, redwood cabins with or without bath, tent cabins (summer only), and housekeeping cabins. The lodge buildings contain a lounge, shops, a cafeteria, a dining room, and a coffee shop.

The Ahwahnee Hotel offers luxurious accommodations in the hotel's main building or in attractive cottages on the hotel grounds. Open the year around except for a short time in December, the Ahwahnee has a gift shop, a cocktail lounge, and an exquisite dining room.

Above the valley floor, rooms with or without bath are available during the summer months at Big Trees Lodge in the Mariposa Grove and at the Wawona Hotel on the Wawona Road 27 miles from the valley. At Tuolumne Meadows there are simple tent cabins and a central canvas-covered dining hall where meals are served family style.

For reservations (always advisable) write to the Yosemite Park and Curry Co., Yosemite National Park, California 95389.

Campgrounds maintained throughout the valley are open from mid-May to mid-September (it's possible to camp the year around); campgrounds in the high country have a shorter season, depending on the snow. To control the camping population in the valley, the total number is restricted to 5,000 persons, and a seven-day camping limit is enforced.

House trailers are accommodated in most campgrounds, but there are no utility hookups except at a private camp at Wawona.

A circle of six High Sierra camps is maintained by

DRAMATIC Yosemite Falls roar over steep granite rocks with full force in spring when snows melt.

GRANITE CLIFFS tower above Yosemite Valley. El Capitan (left) is massive; Half Dome (in distance) looks as if sliced by knife.

AHWAHNEE HOTEL dining room goes informal for winter ski buffets.

Yosemite Park and Curry Company for hikers and saddle parties who wish to enjoy this country with maximum convenience and minimum expense. The camps are about 10 miles apart and consist of dormitory and private tents grouped near a large central dining tent in which you dine family style.

Tuolumne Meadows camp, reached via the Tioga Pass Road, is the only camp in the circuit accessible by automobile. It makes an ideal headquarters for exploring the high country. Other camps are at Merced Lake, Vogelsang, Sunrise, Glen Aulin, and May Lake.

How to enjoy the park

During the summer months, a very active naturalist program is carried on in the park, with campfire programs at Camp Curry, nature walks, lectures, and field trips. The visitor center at Yosemite Village has excellent exhibits explaining the how and why of Yosemite in graphic detail.

An excellent way to see the valley is on bicycle— the roads are mostly level and distances easily ped-

aled. In the summer, you will be bothered by automobile traffic, but during the spring and fall you will have the roads practically to yourself. You can rent bicycles at Yosemite Lodge and Camp Curry.

Another way to tour the valley floor is by open-air motorcoach. On the two-hour tour, you stop at principal viewpoints and park attractions. Cost is $3 for adults, $1.50 for children.

Saddle and pack animals are available at Yosemite Valley stables, Tuolumne Meadows, Wawona, and White Wolf. Also, there are eight packers who pack into Yosemite from strategically located pack stations around the park. For further information, contact High Sierra Packers Association, c/o Bishop Chamber of Commerce, 125 E. Line, Bishop, California.

The more than 700 miles of trails in the park offer every kind of hiking possibility from leisurely walks of an hour or so to trips of a week or longer. The principal waterfalls are good destinations for short hikes from the valley. From Happy Isles a 1-mile trail leads to the base of Vernal Fall and a 3-mile trail takes you to the top of Nevada Fall. Upper Yosemite Falls never ceases to be a wonder. This

HIGH COUNTRY above Yosemite Valley offers packers, hikers, and campers a quiet summer retreat.

WAGON drawn by pair of bell-draped horses tours Yosemite Valley on winter weekends.

hike involves a steep climb from the valley floor to the valley rim. The trail (almost 3½ miles) starts from Camp 4.

Several days a week during the summer, a six-day guided saddle trip leaves Yosemite Valley and makes a circuit of the High Sierra camps, stopping one night in each camp. There is also a four-day saddle trip from Tuolumne Meadows with overnight stops at Glen Aulin, May Lake, and Sunrise camps. If you prefer to hike, there are guided, seven-day hiking trips which leave Yosemite Valley each Sunday during the summer.

Reservations should be made in advance for the guided saddle or hiking trips. For information write to Yosemite Park and Curry Company.

At the south end of Yosemite is the Mariposa Grove of Big Trees. No camping or picnicking is allowed, but you can stroll among about 200 gigantic trees. No private vehicles are allowed into the grove; you enter via a tram system which makes several stops enabling passengers to wander at their own pace. Park naturalists are on duty at Grizzly Giants and the Mariposa Grove museum.

Yosemite in winter

Yosemite Valley is unusually splendid when snow covers it as well as the cliffs and sentinel peaks around it. In this picture-book setting you can enjoy sledding, sleigh rides, and other winter activities against a backdrop of white-etched canyon walls and waterfall courses frosted by frozen mist.

You can rent sleds and snow saucers at Curry Village. The ice skating rink is open daily; rental skates are available.

Sleigh rides (actually rubber-tired wagons drawn by a team of bell-draped horses) start from Yosemite Lodge, circle Ahwahnee Meadows, call at the Ahwahnee Hotel, and then return to Yosemite Lodge. The 1-hour tour operates only on weekends and holidays from 10 A.M. until 3 P.M. and costs $3 for adults, $1.50 for children under 12.

Ski facilities are at Badger Pass, a 20-mile drive from the valley floor. Facilities include a double chair lift, T-bar, day lodge, snack bar, and child care center at the Ski Tots Playhouse.

THE NORTHERN MOUNTAINS

Whiskeytown-Shasta-Trinity Recreation Area
Mt. Shasta • Lava Beds • Lassen

Marble Mountains Wilderness

From the Coast Range east to Nevada and from Redding north to the Oregon border lie the northern mountains, which offer a variety of outdoor recreation. You can fish the Klamath, water-ski on Lake Shasta, hike through the wilderness, swim at Eagle Lake, or camp along mountain streams. At Lava Beds National Monument and Lassen Volcanic National Park, you can see unusual land formations caused by volcanic action.

Interstate 5 is the main north-south route through the northern mountains and State Highway 299, the main east-west route. The highways join at Redding 234 miles north of San Francisco, 173 miles north of Sacramento.

WHISKEYTOWN-SHASTA-TRINITY NATIONAL RECREATION AREA

The Whiskeytown-Shasta-Trinity National Recreation Area, established in 1965 as part of the Federal Bureau of Reclamation's Central Valley Project, consists of three units—Whiskeytown Lake, Shasta Lake, and Clair Engle (Trinity)-Lewiston lakes. All are popular summer destinations with boaters, campers, water-skiers, and picnickers. For detailed information on the recreation area, write to Shasta-Trinity

National Forest, 1615 Continental Street, Redding, California 96001, or to Shasta-Cascade Waterland Association, P.O. Box 1988, Redding, California 96001.

Whiskeytown Lake National Recreation Area

Eight miles west of Redding on State 299 is the Whiskeytown Reservoir, created when the Whiskeytown Dam was constructed to divert water from the Trinity River into the Central Valley. The lake's blue water is good for trout and Kokanee fishing, from either boat or shore. The best time to fish is in fall or early spring. Water-skiing, scuba diving, swimming, and boating are popular because of the 37-mile shoreline with its large and small coves.

There are a number of hiking and riding trails, some of which cross streams or climb high enough to afford fine views of the lake. Hunters usually seek the black-tailed deer, pigeons, quails, or even bears. You can camp and picnic in designated areas, close to the beach. No fires are allowed on the beaches.

The National Park Service maintains a visitor center just off State 299 on the east side of the lake. On the shore of the lake is the Kennedy Memorial,

Fishing, gold panning in Klamath River

Callahan's main street

which commemorates President Kennedy's dedication of the dam and lake in 1963.

Below the dam, Clear Creek (which once produced gold) winds through steep gorges and rocky hills. About 5 miles of the creek's waters are open to trout fishing.

Shasta Lake Recreation Area

Nine miles north of Redding, California's second highest dam, Shasta, serves as the great barrier between the mountains and the valley. The key structure in the Central Valley Project, the dam is 602 feet high and two-thirds of a mile long at its crest.

Self-conducted tours at the base of Shasta Dam show the inner working of the dam, and an exhibit building contains photo and chart explanations of the entire Central Valley Project. Observation points are provided for visitors.

Shasta Lake covers 30,000 acres and has 365 miles of shoreline. It is the largest man-made body of water in the state. Shasta's many arms reach back into the canyons of the Sacramento, McCloud, and Pit rivers, and Squaw Creek.

Shasta Lake is wide and has an unusually placid surface. Resorts on the lake offer swimming, fishing, water sports, and boating. You can charter cruisers or speedboats, or rent boats (with or without motor) by the hour or the day. Also available are self-propelled houseboats which are easy to handle and which give you all the conveniences of a small housekeeping cabin. If you have your own boat, there are ramps at resorts and at several campsites along Shasta's shores. The Forest Service maintains a number of campgrounds around the lake.

The fisherman will find 17 varieties of fish, including German brown, rainbow and Kamloops trout, black bass, Kokanee, and crappie.

Clair Engle (Trinity)-Lewiston lakes

Behind the Trinity Dam, which rises 465 feet, is Clair Engle Lake (Trinity Lake). Situated in the midst of heavily-forested mountains, Clair Engle Lake, has a 145 mile shoreline and 16,500 acres surface waters and offers boating, swimming, fishing, and camping. A visitor center is located 2 miles above Trinity Dam on Buckeye Road.

Lewiston Reservoir, just below Trinity Dam, is at an elevation of about 1,900 feet. It is 7 miles long, very narrow, and resembles a slow-moving river more

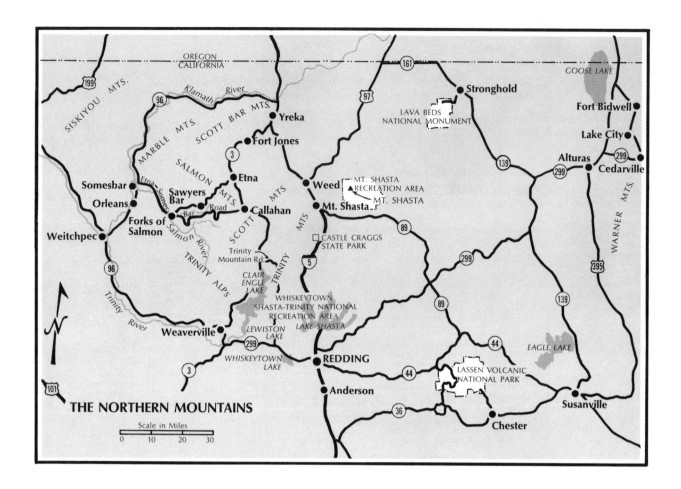

THE NORTHERN MOUNTAINS

Scale in Miles
0   10   20   30

than a lake. Lewiston offers excellent trout fishing. Public boat launching ramps are on the west side of the lake.

TRINITY, SALMON, SCOTT, MARBLE MOUNTAINS

Few access roads lead into the wilderness of the Trinity, Salmon, Scott, and Marble mountains, and only a handful of towns offer accommodations. However, these mountains can be more inviting than the towering Sierra range to the southeast. They are less crowded, generally not as rugged, and more compact, and the high peaks do not have the deep canyons of the Sierra. The rivers and mountain streams offer fishing, and the national forests invite packing and camping.

For information on accommodations, packers, and guides write to Shasta-Cascade Wonderland Association, P.O. Box 1988, Redding, California 96001.

Trinity Alps

The unexpectedly high and rugged Trinity Alps are well screened by lower mountains; you scarcely notice

them driving Interstate 5. An easy approach on cross-mountain State 299 has never brought them heavy traffic.

The Trinity Alps have some striking resemblances to the Sierra. Massive granite peaks sweep up from an alpine highland. Dozens of lakes pocketed in glacial basins feed the outlet creeks and rivers. However, the Trinity Alps are much more compact than the Sierra (trails to the high mountains are shorter), and being closer to coastal moisture, Trinity has proportionately more and fuller streams, greener and thicker underbrush.

Trinity splits the difference between the dry heat of the upper Sacramento Valley and the damp coolness of the Humboldt coast. It has two zones—a low, warmer canyon country and a cool, high mountain wilderness.

The Trinity Alps are a small Mother Lode. Three main roads form a circle around the Alps and link the gold towns. The principal road, State 299, parallels the old Trinity Trail, famous as an Indian path, pioneer trail, and Gold Rush wagon road. The second, State Highway 3, was once part of the main route—the old California-Oregon Wagon Road—north from Shasta to Callahan and Yreka. The third, a dirt road, taps the Salmon River settlements and the north and west slopes (see page 122).

Fishing the Klamath

The Klamath River is not a long river, but it is an impressive stream within cliffed canyons. It offers some of the best steelhead fishing in the state. The Klamath River winds through the mountains from Oregon and heads west to the California coast. Most of the river is paralleled by State Highway 96.

Along the highway river communities offer lodges and resorts. There are several Forest Service campgrounds. For information concerning accommodations and fishing, contact the Klamath, Happy Camp, Klamath River, and Yreka chambers of commerce or the Shasta-Cascade Wonderland Association in Redding.

The most sought-after fish in the Klamath is the steelhead; next in popularity are the sea-going rainbow trout and the salmon. Other migratory fish include coast cutthroat, sturgeon, and shad.

Marble Mountains Wilderness Area

The loop road up the Scott River from Hamburg to Fort Jones and Etna and down the North Fork of the Salmon River to Sawyers Bar, Forks of Salmon, and Somesbar encircles the Marble Mountains—more than 200,000 acres of isolation.

The Marble Mountains are walking mountains and easier to get around in than the Trinity Alps to the south. You have to fight brush along the streams, and the trails are precipitous in places, but for the most part the trails are scenic and easy to follow.

Almost in the exact center of the wilderness area are the Sky High Lakes, which form a hub from which main and spur trails go in all directions. Most of the trails wind through forests of red and white fir, mountain hemlock, western white pine, Douglas fir, black oak and rare weeping spruce.

Packers and hikers use the following as major points of access: Happy Camp, Seiad Valley, and Hamburg on the Klamath; Somesbar at the confluence of the Klamath and the Salmon; Forks of Salmon and Sawyers Bar on the Salmon River; and Etna, Greenview, Fort Jones, and Scott Bar along the Scott River.

Most visitors go into the interior on horseback. You can have the packer leave you at a base camp on a lake and return at a specified date to lead you out. Or the packer can stay with you for the entire trip.

Snow is usually out of the lakes by the middle of June, sometimes not until the first of July. July through September is the best time for the trails.

SCOTT RIVER, tributary of larger Klamath, winds through Scott Mountain wilderness near Fort Jones.

PLACID WATERS of Lake Shasta sparkle behind Shasta Dam, the second highest in California.

THREE DRIVES THROUGH NORTHERN GOLD COUNTRY

The northern mountains had their own Gold Rush explosion, only on a smaller scale than in the Sierra foothills. You can still see evidences of this raucous past on three roads in the Trinity, Salmon, and Scott mountains.

• The Trinity Trail plunges you into Gold Country at the town of Shasta, 6 miles west of Redding on State Highway 299. In October of 1849 Shasta was a tent city of 500 persons. By 1851 it was the diversion point for the shipping of gold by mule train west into the Trinity and north over the Scott Mountains. Shasta was the important city of the north country until the California and Oregon Railroad reached the new town of Redding in 1872.

Today the old "main street" of Shasta is a well kept historic monument. The shells and facades of "the longest row of brick buildings in California" speak for the prosperous past. Only the Old Masonic Hall and the courthouse are complete buildings.

Four miles beyond Shasta is the Whiskeytown Reservoir. Beneath its placid water are the few remains of Whiskeytown, once one of the liveliest

OLD BOTTLES are part of Gold Rush exhibit in museum in Weaverville's history center.

Gold Rush towns in Trinity country. West of the reservoir, the road wanders through dry manzanita and oak foothill slopes, across broad washes, past streams and placer gravel piles, across the Trinity River at Douglas City and on to Weaverville.

A hundred years have brought little change in the frontier-Victorian aspect of Weaverville except for the honey locusts grown tall and the lawns, flowers, and picket fences. At the J. J. "Jake" Jackson Memorial Museum you will see relics of the colorful early days. The Chinese Joss House, a state historical monument, was once a place of worship for the many Chinese who worked the area. The Trinity Historical Park, an attractively landscaped half-acre right next to the red-brick and iron-shuttered museum, has picnic tables, a green lawn, and relics of Weaverville's most famous mines.

From Weaverville, the Trinity Trail follows the Trinity River canyon northwest to Willow Creek for about 60 miles. Along the way you will see evidences of Gold Rush days, in particular the great Oregon Gulch (just south of Junction City), filled to the tree tops with gold-wash sediment.

• To reach Trinity Mountain Road (the old Oregon Wagon Road), turn north off State 299 at Tower House, 16 miles west of Redding. Three miles north of this junction, you will pass French Gulch, a mining town huddling in a canyon. Six miles beyond French Gulch the pavement ends, but an unimproved road will take you over the 4,000-foot Trinity Mountain.

• The Salmon River drive takes you on narrow, winding roads past numerous picnic and fishing spots. State Highway 96 follows the Trinity and Klamath rivers north from Willow Creek 24 miles to Weitchpec, then 16 more miles beyond Orleans where the pavement ends. The Etna-Somesbar Road follows the lonely Salmon River south to Forks of Salmon and then east to Sawyers Bar, a mining camp in the 1850's. Most of its Gold Rush buildings were destroyed in a recent fire.

From Sawyers Bar you cross Russian Creek and continue on a steep grade to the summit of Salmon Mountain. The summit (elevation 5,969 feet) is on a ridge less than 100 feet wide and affords views in every direction.

Descending to agricultural Scott Valley, you meet Interstate 3 at Etna. Twelve miles north of Etna is Fort Jones, established in 1852 for protection of inhabitants against Indian raids. A landmark here is the museum, which contains Indian grinding stones and pestles, millstones from early flour mills, the cornerstone from its first bank, and specimens from the early mines.

SNOW-CAPPED MOUNT SHASTA, volcanic in origin, has elevation of 14,161 feet and is visible for more than one hundred miles. Shasta's heavy coating of snow means a long skiing season.

MOUNT SHASTA AREA

The immense snow-capped peak of Mount Shasta rises to 14,161 feet to dominate the landscape for more than one hundred miles. Volcanic in origin, the huge mountain is composed of two cones: Shasta itself, and Shastina, a small cone which rises from the western flank. Five glaciers mantle the eastern and northeastern flanks above the 10,000-foot level.

Mount Shasta City, on the west side of Strawberry Valley and right at the base of the mountain, was settled in the 1850's. When the Shasta route of the Southern Pacific Railroad reached the settlement in 1886, a townsite was laid out along the railroad. In 1923, the town took the name of the mountain that towers above it.

Mount Shasta Ski Bowl

Mount Shasta normally gets a heavy snow pack, which means skiing often lasts well into spring and in some years goes right through summer. The slopes of the bowl range from a 35 per cent drop in the upper area to 10 per cent in the lower.

Mount Shasta has a double chairlift that takes you to 9,400 feet elevation. There is also a T-bar and two rope tows. A lodge has a cafeteria, cocktail lounge, and ski rental shop. There are no overnight accommodations at the Ski Bowl, but lodging and restaurants are available at Mount Shasta, Weed, and Dunsmuir.

To reach the bowl, leave Interstate 5 at Mount Shasta City, about 60 miles north of Redding, and drive 15 miles east on the Everitt Memorial Highway. This 2-lane road climbs the lower slopes of Shasta in wide curves at a moderate grade.

Lake Siskiyou Recreation Area

Lake Siskiyou, California's newest lake, was constructed solely for recreation purposes. The lake backs up Box Canyon Dam and has a constant-level 430-acre water surface. To reach this recreation area, take the South Fork Road west from Interstate 5 at Mount Shasta.

Shoreline facilities include 50 picnic sites, 245 campsites, a boat ramp, a concession building, and

LASSEN PEAK, which erupted in 1915, looms above devastated area where trees fell away from lava flow.

a sandy beach. Besides swimming and boating, the lake offers good trout fishing.

Castle Crags State Park

A cluster of gray-white granite domes and spires rising out of the evergreen forest 48 miles north of Redding marks the site of Castle Crags State Park, a 3,447-acre reserve straddling Interstate 5 and the Sacramento River.

The principal trail takes you to a prominent cluster of castles west of the highway. To reach them drive up the Kettlebelly Road to its end (about a mile), then follow the trail, which climbs about 1,000 feet in 2½ miles to the foot of Dome. At Indian Springs, a mile from the top, water trickles out of fern-covered rocks. Along the trails many varieties of wildflowers grow, and there are some viewpoints from which you can see Mount Shasta and Lassen Peak, as well as the nearby crags.

LASSEN VOLCANIC NATIONAL PARK

Until May 31, 1914, Lassen Peak's claim to fame was as a landmark for pioneer Peter Lassen, who guided emigrant parties over the mountains and into the Sacramento Valley. Then began the year-long eruptions of smoke, stones, steam, gases, and ashes that culminated in the spectacular events of May 19, 1915. On that day, a red-glowing column of lava rose in the crater and spilled over the sides, melting the snow on the mountain's northeast flank and sending 20-ton boulders and devastating floods of warm mud 18 miles down the valleys of Lost Creek and Hat Creek.

Three days later Lassen literally "blew its top." A column of vapor and ashes rose some 30,000 feet into the sky. A terrific blast of steam and hot gases ripped out the side of the mountain and rushed northeast, killing every living thing in its path for mile after mile. As far away as Reno, Nevada, streets were buried under several inches of ash. Declining eruptions continued into 1917.

On a visit to Lassen today, you will see striking examples of past volcanic activity as well as evidence of present activity.

While much of the Lassen country is accessible only by trail, no point in the park's 163 square miles is more than a day's hike from the road. There are five self-guiding nature trails: at Lily Pond near Manzanita Lake; at Cinder Cone; through Bumpass Hell; at Boiling Springs Lake in Warner Valley; and at Sulphur Works. A leaflet is available which shows key points of interest.

The Lassen Peak Road

The Lassen Peak Road, linked at both ends to State Highway 89, traverses the western part of the park between West Sulphur Creek and Manzanita Lake. It crosses a shoulder of the volcano at 8,512 feet.

At the Sulphur Works Entrance Station, near the park's south boundary, is the most accessible of the hydro-thermal areas—the Sulphur Works Thermal Area. North of here you will pass Brokeoff Mountain, Mount Diller, Mount Connard, and Pilot Pinnacle—peripheral remnants of the much higher Mount Tehama, a huge strato-volcano that collapsed perhaps as recently as a few thousand years ago.

The road crosses the northeast side of Lassen Peak, the area devastated in the 1915 eruptions and now undergoing reforestation. You pass Chaos Crags, hardened pink plugs of thick, pasty lava undercut by steam explosions that caused the rockslides of Chaos Jumbles. A good trail will take you to the top of Lassen Peak. The hike takes about 2 hours and climbs 2,000 feet in 2½ miles from the highway summit. From the highest point, you will see not only the clear-cut evidences of Lassen's 1914-1917 activity, but also the distant Sierra Nevada in the vicinity of

Tahoe, the Coast Range ascending northward to the Trinity Alps, and the icy cone of Mount Shasta.

Lassen Peak Road runs through a devastated area as it approaches Manzanita Lake, main gathering spot of the park. Here are boats for rent, supplies, lodgings, meals. In the Visitor Lodge Center there is a fine assembly of interpretive exhibits.

Biggest and showiest of the thermal areas is Bumpass Hell. Here you will find a natural bowl eaten out of a hard lava rock by hot acids. You will see violently roaring hot springs, boiling muddy pools, crystallined "solfataras," gurgling mud volcanoes, "morning glory" pools, deep turquoise waters over layers of fool's gold, and a mineralized "River Styx."

The Lassen Peak Road closes after the first snow storm until June or July, except in the Lassen Ski Area, just inside the southwest entrance.

The eastern side

From the town of Chester on State Highway 36, two roads enter the western section of Lassen.

On one road you drive 16 miles to Drakesbad (old but comfortable spa, open in summer). The road is unimproved and is rough and dusty in places. At Drakesbad, gateway to the Lassen wilderness, is a 2-mile sign-guided nature trail around Boiling Springs Lake. The trail crosses a meadow and ascends gradually through a forest of pine and fir and through an area of trees killed by an extension of the active thermal area. The lake itself boils and bubbles.

A second road from Chester leads to Juniper and Horseshoe lakes. This road is paved for the first 7 miles; then it is unsurfaced and difficult for large trailers. From Juniper to the end of the road at Horseshoe Lake, the road is steep and rough. Horseshoe Lake is a good base camp for hikes to Snag and Jakey lakes.

Accommodations

The only accommodations within the park are at Manzanita Lake in the northwest corner and at Drakesbad in the southern part of the park.

Manzanita Lake Lodge is open from June 10 (weather permitting) to September 15. The main building contains a curio shop, cocktail lounge, and dining room. The Lodge has a variety of cabins and cottages, including housekeeping units.

Drakesbad Guest Ranch can accommodate 50 in the hotel rooms in the main building.

There are eight campgrounds distributed throughout the park. Four are along the Lassen Park Road— Manzanita Lake, Summit Lake, Kings Creek, and Sulphur Works. Other campgrounds are at Butte Lake, Warren Valley, and Juniper and Horseshoe lakes.

STEAM RISES *from Boiling Springs Lake in Lassen's Drakesbad area. Two-mile trail surrounds bubbling lake.*

THE NORTHEAST CORNER

Scattered throughout the northeast corner of California are Lava Beds National Monument, which has unusual geological formations; the Warner Mountains which offer scenery and solitude; and Eagle Lake for boating and swimming.

Lava Beds National Monument

Just off State Highway 139, almost to the Oregon border, is Lava Beds National Monument. The 46,000-acre area contains startling volcanic features which include 1,500-year-old lava flows, high cinder buttes, and what is probably the world's outstanding exhibit of lava tubes, or lava caves.

The caves were formed long ago by fiery lava streams flowing inside ancient lava flows. As the flows hardened, the inner streams drained, leaving the colorful winding lava caves. Several contain natural ice the year around. Lanterns are provided for self-guided cave explorations.

Other formations include the fire-hardened spatter cones at Fleener Chimneys and Black Crater, the 375-foot-deep Mammoth Crater on the Medicine Lake Road, and many trenches and natural bridges marking collapsed lava tubes.

Prehistoric Indians inhabited this area—as evidenced by the Petroglyph Section of the monument. The trail to Big Painted Cave and Symbol Bridge leads to some of these ancient rock carvings. Canby's Cross and Captain Jack's Stronghold recall the Modoc Indian War of 1872-73.

In the southern section of the park is a campground near monument headquarters.

The Warner Mountains

The topography of the Warner Mountains may bring to mind parts of the Rockies—where unmodified rock strata slant steadily up to a summit ridge and break away abruptly on the other side. The long western slopes of the Warners are carpeted in a random patchwork of pine, aspen, fir, juniper, sage, and grasses.

The Warner Mountains are the water divide between the Great Basin and the Pacific. Their west side streams gather into the Pit River; the short, steep creeks of the eastern scarp are caught and utilized by the ranchers of Surprise Valley before they can be lost in the alkali sinks of Upper, Middle, and Lower Lakes.

There are no resorts or lodges in the Warner Mountains. You can take one-day outings into the high country from Alturas, but if you want to remain in the forest you must camp out.

The only paved road across the Warners is the Cedar Pass route, which descends into Surprise Val-

ley. If you take this road to Cedarville, you can return to U.S. Highway 395 through Fandango Pass on a maintained gravel road. Elsewhere in the Warners, the roads are not maintained.

The Surprise Valley Road joins State 299 at Cedarville and takes you through four villages that recall the 19th century. Cedarville, with a population of about 500, is the biggest and busiest of the towns. Its wood and brick buildings follow the changing levels of the sidewalks, which break off informally into gravel or dirt. Limited accommodations are available. The historic building here is the Bonner Trading Post, a log cabin built in 1865 as a trading post for early immigrants and settlers.

Lake City, 10 miles north of Cedarville, consists of a few old houses clustered around a general store and an old flour mill. The "Lake" part of Lake City is the ghost of an alkaline pond during dry years. But after a year of heavy snows, the pond is filled with water again.

At the valley's northern tip is Fort Bidwell, an Army outpost from 1866 to 1892, and an Indian school for Paiutes from 1892 to 1930. At the southern end of the valley is Eagleville, a wide, shaded place in the road.

The highest part of the Warner Mountains is preserved as a 70,000-acre wilderness where no motor vehicles are permitted and the only signs of civilization are grazing sheep and cattle. Traversing the South Warner Wilderness is the 24-mile long Summit Trail. It hugs the top of the range, first on the west with views to Mount Shasta and Mount Lassen and then briefly on the east where you look down cliffs onto the neat pattern of ranches in Surprise Valley 4,000 feet below. The trail leads through rocky flats with patches of snow, and down into meadows with wildflowers. It skirts the three highest peaks—Squaw (8,646 feet), Warren (9,711 feet), and Eagle (9,889 feet). All are climbable.

Off Summit Trail to either side are trails to some fine trout fishing, especially in Pine, Mill, and East creeks and South Emerson Lake. Trout in the Warners are not large, but they are plentiful. The side trails lead to secondary roadheads which you can take to shorten your trip.

It takes 2 or 3 days to hike the entire Summit Trail. From the south the trail starts at Patterson Meadow, 42 miles by car from Alturas. The trail ends at Pepperdine Camp, 20 miles east of Alturas.

Eagle Lake

Eagle Lake, an irregularly-shaped body of water 13 miles long and up to 4 miles wide, is the second largest natural lake entirely within California. Though at a high elevation (5,100 feet), its waters are warmed by the sun to a comfortable 70° in summer,

WESTERN JUNIPER grows among dry, black lava remnants at Lava Beds. Plant, animal life is plentiful despite rugged terrain.

RIDGE of Warren Peak backs up Patterson Lake in Warner Mountains.

and are good for swimming, water-skiing, and boating. Eagle Lake sports good trout fishing. The lake's waters are quite alkaline, though not enough to bother swimmers or the trout.

The lake lies across the line marking the abrupt end of Lassen National Forest's pine-studded uplands and the beginning of the semi-arid southern portion of the Modoc Plateau. The lake can be reached by Eagle Lake Road 3 miles west of Susanville, or via Heart Failure Grade off State 139.

Along the south shores heavy stands of pine and fir surround lush mountain meadows. Off in the distance you can see some of the northeastern half of the lake and its contrasting shores of sagebrush, rock, and sagebrush-dotted sand dunes.

Gallatin Beach on the southern end of the lake is a recreation center. Here you will find a marina and concessioners. Nearby are Forest Service camp-

grounds, picnic areas, and a long swimming beach.

From the Gallatin Beach area you can travel around the west side of the lake on a partly paved, partly dirt road. You pass ice caves and cinder pits on your way to Spaulding Tract where there are summer homes, an airstrip, and campgrounds. A fish trap has been built here to catch the spawning Eagle Lake trout in early spring. Just to the west of the trap are several Indian ruins, circles of rock walls about 10 feet in diameter.

At the north end of Eagle Lake there are a number of beaches covered with the colorful shells of small mollusks that thrive in the fertile water. A variety of wildlife can be found on the lake and on its shores.

For more detailed information about Eagle Lake write to the Lassen County Chamber of Commerce, P.O. Box 338, Susanville, California 96130.

Index

The following organizations will be happy to provide additional information on the areas covered in this book:

THE ASSOCIATION OF METROPOLITAN SAN JOSE, 165 West San Carlos St., San Jose 95114; BUTTE COUNTY DEVELOPMENT COMMISSION, 175 Cohasset Road, Chico 95926; CALAVERAS COUNTY CHAMBER OF COMMERCE, Box 177, San Andreas 95249; CARMEL VALLEY CHAMBER OF COMMERCE, Box 217, Carmel Valley 93924; FORT BRAGG-MENDOCINO COAST CHAMBER OF COMMERCE, Box 1141, Fort Bragg 95437; FRESNO CHAMBER OF COMMERCE, Box 1469, Fresno 93716; GREATER NORTH LAKE TAHOE CHAMBER OF COMMERCE & CONVENTION BUREAU, Box 884, Tahoe City 95730; HUMBOLDT COUNCIL CHAMBERS OF COMMERCE, County Courthouse, Eureka 95501; LAKE COUNTY CHAMBER OF COMMERCE, Box 517, Lakeport 95453; LAKEPORT TOURIST BUREAU, Box 115, Lakeport 95453; LASSEN COUNTY CHAMBER OF COMMERCE, Box 338, Susanville 96130; MARIN COUNTY CHAMBER OF COMMERCE & VISITORS BUREAU, 824 5th Ave., San Rafael 94901; MENDOCINO COUNTY CHAMBER OF COMMERCE, Box 244, Ukiah 95482; MONTEREY PENINSULA VISITORS & CONVENTION BUREAU, Monterey 93940.

NEVADA COUNTY CHAMBER OF COMMERCE, 244 Commercial St., Nevada City 95959; OAKLAND CHAMBER OF COMMERCE CONVENTION & TOURISM BUREAU, 1320 Webster St., Oakland 94612; OROVILLE AREA CHAMBER OF COMMERCE, Oroville Inn, Oroville 95965; PACIFIC GROVE CHAMBER OF COMMERCE, Box 167, Pacific Grove 93950; PLUMAS COUNTY CHAMBER OF COMMERCE, Box 1018, Quincy 95971; SACRAMENTO METROPOLITAN CHAMBER OF COMMERCE, Box 1017, Sacramento 95805; SAN FRANCISCO CONVENTION & VISITORS BUREAU, Fox Plaza, San Francisco 94102; SANTA CRUZ COUNTY CONVENTION & VISITORS BUREAU, Box 921, Santa Cruz 95060; SHASTA-CASCADE WONDERLAND ASSOCIATION, Box 1988, Redding 96001; SONORA PASS VACATIONLAND, Box 607, Columbia 95310; SOUTH LAKE TAHOE CHAMBER OF COMMERCE, Box 3418, South Lake Tahoe 95705; TUOLUMNE COUNTY CHAMBER OF COMMERCE, Box 277, Sonora 95370.